FIRSTMATTERPRESS
Portland, Ore.

ALSO BY K. M. LIGHTHOUSE

You Are An Ambiguous Pronoun

The Observer Effect

TIME COUNTS BACKWARD FROM INFINITY

k.m. lighthouse

FIRSTMATTERPRESS
Portland, Ore.

Published in the United States
by First Matter Press
Portland, Oregon

Paperback ISBN 978-0-9972987-7-2

Book design & typography
by Ash Good www.ashgood.design

FIRSTMATTERPRESS.ORG

For my dad.
May your healing be continual.

TIME COUNTS BACKWARD FROM INFINITY

"WHAT DOES 343 MEAN TO YOU?"

"What?"

"The tattoo on your hand?"

"Oh, it's just a number that's been following me around for the last 10 years or so."

"You, too, huh? I know this is going to sound crazy, but when you sat down next to me on the bus, it was some wild déjà vu when I saw that number. I was in a real bad way a while ago, and that number, I feel like it healed me. It felt like God was talking to me or some shit. I know that sounds crazy, but it's true. Was it like that for you, too?"

I look over at the window before refocusing on the stranger's face.

"I don't know what it means yet. It was the exit I took for my first job, my locker number, the number on my plane tickets, website logins, the time I wake up in the middle of the night. But I don't know what it means. I wanted to make it my own omen."

"Did you know it's seven cubed? It's God's number. Three hundred and forty-three firefighters died in 9/11. There's even a Facebook page for people who have been seeing it everywhere. I mean, what other number has a Facebook page? And the individual numbers add up to 10, and if you take the individual numbers, you can write them in a function to get—"

"It's the speed of sound at room temperature. And, sometimes, it feels like a name."

"Want to just start at the beginning?" the university therapist asks.

"I keep . . . well, I'm hearing these voices in my head?"

"What do they say to you?"

"It's difficult to hear the words. It's just a garbled mess."

"Your dad is going to play a song at the funeral, and F is doing the program design. I thought it would be nice if you wrote a poem about your brother and read it. So we don't have to use something generic. We could put it on the back of the program."

"The funeral, it's in a week, right?" I ask.

"If you can't do it, that's all right. I just thought you might want to."

"I don't think you'd want the poem I would write."

"I didn't know they made caskets that small."

"I'm worried about John. He just got clean, and then . . . then this happened. I reached out to his sponsor, but I haven't heard back."

"I have no idea how to help my dad," I say. "Did you know he punched a hole in the hospital wall?"

"Yeah, didn't they put a painting over the hole?"

"I don't think Dad's okay. He keeps saying he's just trying to come down off the pain medication. Do you know what that's about?"

"He went to Mexico to get his teeth replaced."

"All of them?"

"Well, he didn't have many left. They pulled out all the ones he had and replaced them with porcelain implants. He's been on serious pain medication ever since."

"Why'd he go down there?"

"It's cheaper, I guess."

"Oh, he just sent me another picture."

"I'm not in a good way, sweetheart, but I need company," Dad says.

"Do you want me to come now?"

"Yes. When you get here, we can go see the fish. You know, at the aquarium?"

"Do you need me to stop and grab anything?"

"Two packs of Marlboro 100s."

I purchase those and a pack for myself, smoking my first cigarette on the drive over.

On the way to Newport, I sing:

Up on Cripple Creek, she sends me
If I spring a leak, she mends me
I don't have to speak, she defends me
A drunkard's dream if I ever did see one

The song sounds wrong every time I get to "drunkard's dream." Dad could never get those chords right. How many times had I heard him repeat that as a kid?

∞

“I am the storm today.”

“Ride your winds; channel your lightning.”

I brave this cabin with its vaulted ceilings and an old man's blood on the walls. No one answers the door when I knock, but I hear voices around back and know Dad is there.

I navigate the kitchen with its forest of empty liquor bottles, one of them proudly displaying the Trump brand. I cringe. The empty bottle alone is probably worth more than any vodka I'd ever pay for. Despite the generous counter space, the bottles fight for real estate with dishes caked with rotting food and half-empty cans of soup.

“Are you okay, Dad? Dad?”

I'm in a room with gray walls. It's small with sparse furniture. I'm not alone. Someone is here, standing in the corner wearing colors that blend into the room. The lightless interior gives the face a gray pallor.

"Are you ready?"

"Yes," I hear myself say.

"Are you sure? I need you to be sure."

"*Yes*," I say.

The room begins decompiling with the grating, glitchy sound of a faulty DVD player. The other person begins to decompile as well, their face coming apart vertically until I'm alone in the dark.

I open my eyes.

"Are you okay, Dad? Dad?"

"Just coming down off my pain medication, baby girl. Haven't shot up for three days. Don't you worry about me."

The phone rings on the tempered glass table. He hands it to me and says, "tell them I'm okay."

When I found him, unaccustomed to his teeth,
lips sunken, tongue searching out
the foreign bodies hammered into his head,

he had a Packers blanket around his shoulders
but no shoes, no socks.
He shouted to the trees,

"We killed it! We killed it! My god, we killed it."
There were so many trees to tell.
Marijuana buds, orange Gatorade,

three dozen cigarette butts, two Bud Light Clamatos.
There was an empty chair,
but I was standing.

"Listen, we didn't miss a single note. Just three of us
and all three floors. We killed it!
Prince just died, you know. Let's show her the one . . . "

This was the peeling of the vegetable man. This was
the burning off of decay, hard and fast.
He was coming in low and fast, riding the waves

of PTSD from a plane he never flew.
He wasn't alone, but Pops, who
praised the lord at my arrival, could have been

the other half of Dad's personality disorder, a phantom,
indoctrinated, nameless, making a good show
of being at least half as broken.

And perhaps, as a society, we need substances such as alcohol, a collective allowance so to speak, a space where we can tolerate these social trespasses so we have something else to blame the behavior on when our cognitive dissonance becomes too great.

"Thank god. Oh, thank god," Pops says. "You don't know what it's been like, what it's been like. Been up for three days. Slept in a diesel truck that night! Ain't that right?"

"Tell it like it is, brother. Say it for the whole congregation. We sure have been livin'," Dad says.

"Damn right. We've been treetop fliers!" Pops agrees. "I shouldn't have said the thing about the cello."

"We got into a little bit of a fight, throwing fists, and afterward, I was runnin' around trying to find him. Oh man, lured Pops into a hug, and I don't know why, but I wanted to throw him off the deck, and it was rainin'. Slipped on some of his blood in my cowboy boots. That's the only thing that snapped me out of it. Probably would have killed the son of a bitch. Look, there's still some blood on the wall. I cleaned most of it up."

"Ah, but you ain't mean nothing by it. You didn't find me in the diesel truck. No sir."

"And I looked for several hours, too."

Away from my dad, Pops tells me, "You have to help me. I haven't slept. *He* won't sleep!" The eerie smile on Pops' face wavers like melted plastic. His sunglasses make it impossible to read his eyes.

John: I'm recording now, guys. You're on tape! Let's play some music. We've got a full band here tonight! Yes, sir. We've got a...a...well, I've got the guitar, and I'm singin', then there's R with another guitar, Pops on the sax, and Dubs on the cello! We got a real live cello here, folks! Let's make him feel welcome... [John lowers his voice] ...because he's real shy.

R: Let me just finish my drink here.

John: We can drink when we're dead.

Pops: We almost *were* dead after this weekend, huh?

John: Born survivors! All right, let's start up with "Purple Rain." Fade in the cello first, Dubs.

Dubs: Me? Oh, right.

[soft cello sounds vaguely to the tune of "Purple Rain"]

Pops: Goddamn. That sounds like shit.

[cello stops]

Dubs: You know what, R? I'm just going to go. I'll see you 'round.

R: He didn't—oh, all right. See you 'round.

John: You can't just leave! Prince just died! We need you, man.

Dubs: No, I'm leaving. You guys have a good time.

[zipper sounds]

[fireplace crackles]

[door closes]

John: Goddamn it, Pops!

Pops: I'm sorry, John. I've had a couple drinks is all.

John: You're a fuckin' alcoholic. Got me started on this shit again. I'm going to... I'll fuckin' kill you for that. I just... I wanted a cello in the recording. And now all we have is your goddamn sax.

Pops: Come off it, man, you don't mean that.

John: Let’s just start over. R, you start.

[guitar chords]

John: Yeah! Yeah!

[saxophone]

John: Wait, wait, let’s do this like a proper recording. Use all three floors! R, you head up onto the balcony. Pops, you go downstairs. I’ll do the recording from here.

R: I really don’t think...

John: Just fuckin’ do it, R.

[footsteps going up and downstairs]

John: Let’s start again. For the whole congregation!

[muffled guitar and sax sounds]

John: *I never meant to cause you any sorrow. Never meant to cause you any pain...*

"We flew up so fast from the Gulf of Mexico, drove straight through to Wyoming and then straight over to here, snowin' all the way here, and you wonder why they're thinkin' I'm crazy. Got no sleep. Got no sleep! And then there was that car crash at four in the morning. I got to the guy before the police did, pulled him out of that truck, and the son-of-a-bitch's scalp flopped over his face. Pops passed out on the way to the emergency room, but the guy made it out to the hospital all right. He made it all right."

Dad says, “Lemme tell you what kind of man R is. He likes this. He likes that he can be so close to this excitement, to this crazy, but he can go home. He has a wife, kids, yeah, sure. But this is what he lives for. Me comin’ ’round all fucked up and shit. This is what he lives for.”

R says, "I love your dad, Kassandra, don't get me wrong. He's been a good friend to me, but he could have killed a man. I live in this town. I don't want police in my house. Where would I be then? Where would I be then?"

"You gotta listen to this, baby girl. Are you hearing this? We fuckin' killed it." The self-recorded cover drones on from the Bluetooth speaker and still I can hear his yelling. "I really wanted that cello, man. I really wanted it. God, this tooth really hurts. I didn't know pain could feel like this."

"That one looks like it could be infected."

"Oh, but you have to listen to this part. Listen." He turns up the speaker. I didn't realize it could go louder.

"We're looking for an emergency dentist in the area. You're going to be all right."

"They're not going to help me. Nobody's helping me. I need to go to the emergency room."

"Let's see if we can get you an appointment first."

"WHY WON'T ANYBODY HELP ME? Am I so much of a bad guy?"

"We *are* . . . We are trying to help."

"Then take me to the goddamned hospital."

Pops says, “Not once was I scared with her behind the wheel, but *damn* was she doin’ 80 ’round them curves.”

"I'm going to die! I'm going to die! I'm going to die! Kill me! Just kill me now!"

"Sir . . ."

"This plane is coming in low and fast! Low and fast!"

"Sir, we need you to fill out some paperwork."

"I can do it. I'm his daughter."

"Kassandra, Kassandra, you can do it for me right? You know how to kill me?"

"Does he have insurance?"

"No, he's paying out of pocket."

"I see."

When I look up from the paperwork, Dad is holding the hand of a middle-aged woman. She's comforting him, and I want to apologize, but the nurse pulls my attention back.

"He'll need to take these antibiotics twice daily, and we've prescribed him some oxycodone. Don't let him take more than four of these a day. And keep him from drinking. He'll need to take this one on an empty stomach and take this one after he's eaten something. Can you sign . . . "

You'd have to be the damn patient to be a good enough doctor. And even then you're still playing God.

He tells me to kill him. Or rather,
yells it in the emergency room.
He says, "I want to die like a man, not like a bitch,"

but I never learned what a man was.
He asks me if I know how to kill him gently,
before the plane crashes.

"Why won't anyone see me? Why won't they
see me? Am I so much of a bad guy?"
But, "at least—at least," he tells me,

"Newport is a beautiful place to die."
His head slumps forward when I stop
holding it up. But then he sits upright, looks at me,

and asks, "Do you think we could still see the fish?"
I find myself laughing, a disembodied, hollow sound.
There are too many of us in the triage room.

Blood pressure? Fine.
Pulse? Normal.
Oxygen levels? Stable.

"Just pain? I'm not dying—it's just pain?
Then I'm gonna have a cigarette."
He stands and waltzes through automatic doors

to settle near the no-smoking sign.
This is what they meant
when they said to choose your battles.

I could have killed him. But no, he's lived 80 years
in half the time, and I'm asking for more.
He has more deserts to cross, more

planes to land. So, we go back,
butt-shot numb for six hours.

He pops two of the pills into his mouth and swallows without water. I try to keep track of the bottle. Had I set it down on the counter?

"You'll have to make sure I keep breathing." I shake my head and move into the kitchen. I scrape furiously at some days-old dishes in the sink, and when I turn to put the pan on the drying rack, Dad takes a swig from a fifth of vodka.

"Hadn't he been sober for years?"

"That's what he told me, anyway."

∞

It is a mistake to believe that circles will not reconnect, to forget that a count-up is also a countdown.

"Do you ever get the feeling that the consciousness you have now isn't the one you've always had? Like, maybe there are points in your life when a different consciousness arrives and accesses the memories and cognitive tools and plans of the old consciousness and picks right back up where the other left off?"

"Like playing a video game?"

∞

I open my eyes and remember that someone told me the veil between worlds is thinnest between three and four in the morning. I wonder if that is what is happening to me.

I return to my stupor and am pulled deep into my body, into the blackness punctuated by the prismatic tendrils of my nervous system. I hear a set of seven tones. Five of the tones are the same note, but the second and sixth note rise on the scale. The tones continue.

Repeat. Repeat.

The sound is not unpleasant.

Repeat. Repeat.

The rhythm of the seven tones remains steady even though my brain speeds up music, especially when I can't sleep. I open my eyes to make sure I am still awake.

When I close my eyes again, the sound of my body is still there. The tones correspond to places on this physical form, so I investigate my throat. The right side of my throat has little feeling, so I ask the nerve tendrils to readjust. I move to investigate the area of my uterus. I listen close for places requesting attention. I am drawn to my left ovary, which feels disconnected from the rest. I want to improve the blood supply, so I do some rearranging.

The tones all sound the same note now and condense into a vibration. It sounds healthy. I fall asleep to the sound.

In the morning, the place where my thighs touch is covered in menstrual blood, but I manage to keep the sheets clean.

∞

"What does 343 mean to you?"

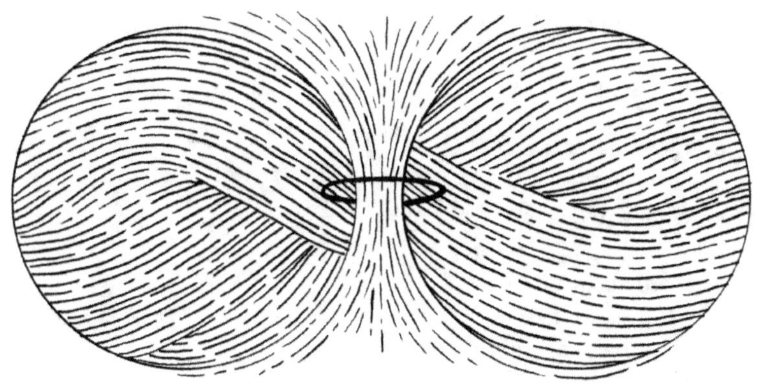

“Want to just start at the beginning?” the university therapist asks.

“I keep . . . well, I’m hearing this voice in my head? It’s a woman’s voice.”

“Does she have a name?”

“Eve. Just Eve.”

“What does she say?”

“‘You will arrive at 1:43.’”

“Does that time have any significance to you?”

“It’s the time I was born.”

"Your dad is going to play a song at the funeral, and F is doing the program design. I thought it would be nice if you wrote a poem about your brother and read it. So we don't have to use something generic. We could put it on the back of the program."

"The funeral, it's in a week, right?" I ask.

"If you can't do it, that's all right. I just thought you might want to."

"I'll think about it."

"Don't let him backslide, okay? My dad just got clean, and then . . . then this happened. I'm just worried about him."

"Look, I've been in contact with his sponsor. John's stronger now than he was then. His son is still so young. At the very least, he has to keep going for the kid. I have complete faith in him."

∞

"I'm not in a good way, sweetheart, but I need company."

"Do you want me to come now?"

"Yes. When you get here, we can go see the fish."

"Do you need me to stop and grab anything?"

"Two packs of Marlboro 100s."

I make the mistake of purchasing the cigarettes early in the drive. They sit in the passenger seat, tempting me. If it weren't for the plastic wrap, he wouldn't have known what was missing.

"Thank god. Oh, thank god," Pops says. "You don't know what it's been like, what it's been like. Been up for three days. Slept in a diesel truck that night! Ain't that right?"

"Tell it like it is, brother. Say it for the whole congregation. We sure have been livin'," Dad says.

"I really wanted that cello, man. I really wanted it. God, this tooth really hurts. I didn't know that pain could feel like this."

"We're trying to get you an appointment. Will you be able to wait?"

"WHY WON'T ANYBODY HELP ME? Am I so much of a bad guy?"

"We *are* . . . We are trying to help."

"Then take me to the goddamned hospital."

"He'll need to take these antibiotics twice daily, and we've prescribed him some high-dose ibuprofen since you requested that we not give him any opiates. Don't let him take more than four of these a day. And keep him from drinking. He'll need to take this one on an empty stomach and take this one after he's eaten something. Can you sign . . . "

"I don't even know if the pain was real. Maybe I was just jonesin'.
I don't want to know what I'll feel like when this shot wears off."

"You're gonna have to make a choice, baby girl. Here's the thing: I need to sleep. I haven't slept in three days. I can either get to drinking to put me out or I can take one or two of these." Dad holds up a prescription bottle addressed to Pops.

"What are they?"

"They're for alcohol withdrawal. Little things'd kill a two year old, but I'll be fine. I'll take a couple of 'em, and they'll put me to sleep."

"You can't drink while you take the antibiotics."

"Is that your final answer?"

"I . . ." I sigh. "Sure." Dad pops two of the pills into his mouth and swallows without water.

"You'll have to make sure I keep breathing, then."

∞

"If it weren't true, it might be funny," I say.

"You know, all this would make a great book."

It's finally time, the

Stars have

"It's almost hard to feel sorry when things like this happen to a writer. You know they're just gonna write it into a book anyway."

lined up—I am going to take

the time to

"Are you going to put that in a book?"

write my
book. I
know
and have
observed

"What if you just wrote it down?"

your great talents in this

arena. Would you

"Have you tried writing it down?"

help your old man and keep

"Put that in the book."

him on task?

Here's my note from the Author:

Despite the

left or right
T was elected president

I don't so much care about your

echo chamber

"News"

but

if you look in the mirror and see both the problem and the solution
this

will liberate you.

Write the book.
Write the book.
Write the book.
Write the book.
Write the book.
Write the book.
Write the book.
Write the book.
Write the book.
Write the book.
Write the book.
Write the book.
Write the book.
Write the book.
Writethebook.
Writhe
Write
write
rite
rite
rite
rite
rit
it
i

Up against the door of Dad's bedroom, listening to the sounds of his sleep apnea, I speak with Eve.

"Tell me a happy story about John. There has to be one."

"There were. There are. There's, well . . . "

"You can't think of one?"

"There's a hole there, in my memory. Like my brain doesn't want me to remember. Or thinks it never happened."

∞

When I am nine years old, he teaches me to build a fire in the hearth of our home. I can build and maintain a fire before I know how to cook. Dad asks me for advice before I know how to argue. I practice my words before I say them.

The first year Dad lives in an apartment away from Mom, we spend Christmas with him. We pick out a Christmas tree and buy blue and silver ornaments from the Walmart one mile west. My youngest sister puts Walmart smiley face stickers on all the round ornaments.

When Christmas is over, Dad carries the tree to the field behind the complex and lights it on fire while we watch. My sister can't stop staring at the orb that is level with her eye, sticker facing forward, smile melting at the edges.

I shake my head, frustrated.

"I don't know why we're doing this. I don't know why we're going back the way we came."

"What do you mean?"

"This same reality. The one we came from. We're going back."

When Eve doesn't respond, I continue, "You know how, in the *Nightmare Before Christmas*, Jack finds all the holiday doors?"

"I've never seen it."

"It felt like we were choosing which reality to go back to just now. And we went back through the door we came through in the first place. We went back to Halloween Town."

Eve stares at me but does not speak.

"It was there! Everything was there! All the answers were there, and we went back the way we came."

"There are other ways to find it. I promise. That feeling isn't going away." Eve kisses the top of my head, and I begin to calm down.

"I don't want to forget."

"I will help you remember."

Shamans in all times and places gain their power through relationships with helping spirits, which they sometimes call ancestors, which they sometimes call nature spirits. But somehow the acquisition of a relationship to a disincarnate intelligence is the precondition for authentic shamanism. Now, nowhere in our world do we have an institution like that—that we do not consider pathological—except in the now very thinly spread tradition of the muse. That artists—alone among human beings—are given permission to talk in terms of "my inspiration," or "a voice which told me to do this," or "a vision that must be realized." The thin line—the thin thread of shamanic descent into our profane world—leads through the office of the artist. And so, if society is to somehow take hold of itself at this penultimate moment, as we literally waver on the brink of planetary extinction, then the artist like Ariadne following her thread out of the labyrinth, is going to have to follow this shamanic thread back through time.

“Hey, I want to do something kinda weird, but just go with it, okay? It’s like a rebirth ceremony. For your new name. It’ll give you some more mileage.”

I nod while my friend gathers other friends and my head swims from the half-pan of THC-infused Rice Krispies.

He places me on the ground in the center of four people as they hold hands around me. I feel Eve’s body next to mine, and my forehead rests against familiar knees.

I hear someone volunteer to be the vagina, and then I know what this is: an artificial womb, a spanking machine. I want to reach for Eve’s hand but can’t find it. I inhale the breath of the friend nearest me; I have forgotten her name.

The people who comprise the womb start to squeeze. Inside the ball of bodies, the squeezing grows intense, forcing me up and out of the artificial womb, but we cannot both go through the line of legs simultaneously. I go first.

As I travel through the birthing canal, the hands of my friends slap me, but I barely feel them. I begin to cry. I want to stop, but the hands propel me forward, and the legs are so tight around me that I cannot look behind to make sure Eve is following. I crawl on the carpet through time, through all the time I spent without Eve, through all the darkness of the primordial liquid I swam through to find her.

I climb hands and knees through time and its chasm of loneliness, through kaleidoscopes of organic machine parts. I crawl through 10 sets of legs, but the line keeps going. I leave wet spots in the shape of my tears. My lungs are gasping bits of inner tube. I see the light at the end, but it's blurred by strings. The strings are filled with light or maybe made out of it, but I pass right through them. No, not strings—webs. I see where they connect between my friends, and not just now but also in eternity. I see a failed business venture. I see the whale songs of an oceanographer I will know three years from now. I see the fabrications of the transient storyteller, and I know I will ask him to leave.

Two of my friends sit back-to-back to simulate a cervix before the final set of legs. I pry them apart, though my strength is depleted, and crawl through the vagina to collapse on the orange-brown carpet. Finally, I turn around. I see Eve. She has come out after me. There was nowhere else to go, but there is nowhere else she wants to be. I cling to her and do not leave my place on the carpet for two hours while I wait for my friends to disperse in the afterbirth.

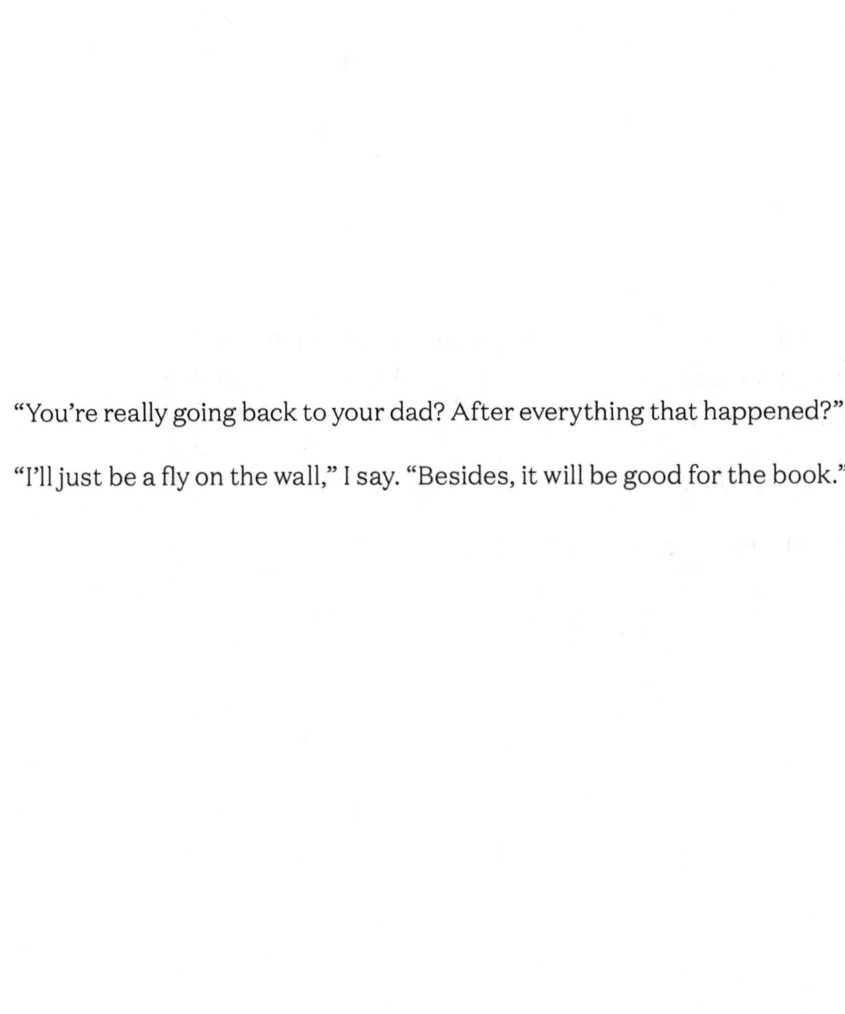

“You’re really going back to your dad? After everything that happened?”

“I’ll just be a fly on the wall,” I say. “Besides, it will be good for the book.”

"He has pictures of me on his phone. So many pictures. He keeps sending them to me. Can you delete them? He doesn't . . . he shouldn't have them anymore."

"I don't . . . he usually has his phone on him. How would I . . . ?"

"Just think about it, okay? Just in case?"

∞

"If I'm going to travel with you and write the book with you, if I'm going to do any of this with you," I say, back on the porch of the cabin, "then I need you to ask before you touch me. I already have a tenuous grasp on my body, and your manic energy makes it worse."

"I can do that. That's fair," he says. There, I had it; my first-ever boundary with a man. How fitting to create it with the first man to see me outside the womb.

"Hey! Yeah, get over here. Come meet Kassandra."

"Hi," I say, shaking the lumber grader's hand.

"Your oldest daughter, I presume?"

"Yep. The writer with a bachelor's degree. Did I tell you she got a full-ride scholarship? Meal plan, dorm, and everything? Fuckin' brilliant, this one."

"No, I don't believe you did. Nice to meet you." I nod warily, uncomfortable with the praise. "Your dad, he's been so good to me. Got me this job here about, what, has it been five years, John?"

"Damn right."

"You're lucky to be his daughter, Kassandra, if you're half as smart as he is."

"I have to go back to Mexico, Kassandra. They're the only ones who can fix this tooth. All these teeth."

"There are plenty of dentists here."

"They told me they wouldn't help me again if Americans touched my teeth."

"What's this really about, Dad?"

"I met someone down there. At La Puerta Verde. She used to be a dolphin trainer, but she got deported from Nicaragua back to Mexico. She had kids there. I bought her out of her contract at La Puerta Verde for three months. She had to pick up work where she could find it, you know? All those girls down there, but I picked this one. Bought her out of her contract so I'm her only client. I miss her. I love her."

"What about your wife, Dad?"

"In Mexico, I didn't orgasm once. I kept that for her. At least I can give her that. But I have to call. I miss this girl like crazy. She's the only person who's going to make me feel better. I have to call her."

"Why are you telling me this?"

"I need to call her. I need . . . Look, I need to call her. I just need to talk to her."

He dials the number and hands it to me. A woman answers.

"Bueno."

I stare at him blankly.

"What's she saying? Can you translate for us?" he asks.

"¿Entiendes, mi hermana?"

If it weren't true, it would have been funny.

The monkeys
they laugh because it hurts so much.

“I have discovered the art of bending time.”

“Por favor, mija, aprendame.”

“Enséñame,” I correct.

He does not walk
across the desert of withdrawal;

he takes a plane. He flies without directions
on an empty tank,

voice wavering through turbulence
as he yells, “Let’s go see the fish!” into the headset.

Reality’s plane was out of commission,
so he chose another dimension, prepared

to crash-land into the mountains
where he buried his soul or maybe my first dog;

I can’t remember.
He is always headed to the ocean,

and when I meet him there, we both
stand over cliffs. There are no fish in the desert.

This is MAGI 1, over.

At the aquarium, he becomes transfixed
by jellyfish and leaves me with the sharks.

The ghost of him yells, “$20 to whoever finds the eel first!”
But I look, and suddenly

the money doesn’t matter
and then the eel doesn’t matter either as we sink

into the oblivion
of what we thought was ocean.

"We did it; we landed the plane," he keeps telling me.

"Do you know how much I hate TV? I put *bullets* in a hotel TV in Mexico!"

Pops tells him, "You don't need to go puttin' bullets in the TV. I turned the thing off. I turned the thing off."

"You asked me a question, and when I told you the answer, you were staring at the damn TV! You didn't even fuckin' *hear* me!"

"It won't happen again. I swear it won't."

"The next time, it *will* be bullets, you ungrateful piece of shit. You listen to me when I talk to you."

"If I'm going to stay with you, I'm not going to stand around and let you talk to Pops like that."

"What do you mean?"

"You know what I mean. You know what? Without him, you're just some dude with a guitar. You need him and his sax, but you don't want him to know how good he is. You don't want him to know that he's better than you are. So you treat him like shit. You treat him like shit, and you tell him he's worthless. That he'd be nowhere without you. I won't stand here and watch that happen."

"'Some dude with a guitar.'" He laughs hollowly.

"Just . . . just leave him alone, all right?"

"Okay," he says, putting a hand on my shoulder as I turn around to go inside. "Sorry," he adds after I flinch.

"I can't touch my own fucking daughter?"

"Remember that blonde from the bank? I invited her out tonight. I bet you a dime she'll be at this open mic. Even though she's got a boyfriend. She'll be here. Videotape this one, Kassandra. We can put it in the book."

He swaps out the stage mic and puts down his guitar.

"So happy to be here, Newport, standing up here with these guys, been too long on the road. We're the MAGI, and we've got a CD comin' out here soon. Been too long on the road, and we're startin' to get real sick of each other. But, here we are, inauguration night, all them women in Portland marchin' and protestin' and whatnot. I voted for the guy. Can we get some more volume?"

A woman in a red dress takes off one red sock and throws it up on stage, and someone else yells, "shut up and play the damn guitar!"

"We're gettin' there, right? We're gettin' there. This is my dad's mic, you know? He used to bring me, I was eight years old, and he would bring me to his shows at the bar. I would, you know, drink a little soda and listen to him sing the blues. Those goddamn blues. Ain't that what we're all here for? Yeah, that's right. That's right. I'm a love supporter! I'm a Trump supporter!"

"Your time's up," the hostess says.

He jumps from the stage and slams the unisex bathroom door.

“I live my life on the street the way other people live theirs in the closet,” he says.

"It occurs to me that I don't even know your real name," I say.

"Seriously, kiddo? I don't even like the name 'Pops.' It's just something your dad started calling me after he helped me move to Wyoming and get my own apartment. I ain't very good with money. He helped me get clean back then, you know. Was closer to me than my sponsor. My real name's Dane."

For the price of rent, you can steal a name.

Wide Sargasso Sea *references supernatural stories from the West Indies about raising the dead, during which the sorcerer would give a new name to the risen body. This person would be called a "zombi," which the book defines as either "a dead person who seems to be alive or a living person who is dead." Likewise, by renaming a person, it is possible to control them. The protagonist's recent husband renames her "Bertha" when he begins to tire of her. Later, referencing this same idea, Antoinette says, "There are always two deaths; the real one and the one people know about."*

"What'll it be, Sunday?" the bartender asks him.

"Sunday?"

"Yeah, you, with the Taking Back Sunday shirt."

"Hey, I kinda like that. 'Sunday.' I could get used to that. I'm taking back Sunday. What d'you think, Kassandra?"

He burns his boots and his name in a graveyard he breaks into. He puts an ace of spades between them for good measure, accessories for the camera. He hangs two of the photographs in his apartment, and I swear I can see a face in the flames.

He drives away in the rental car, and I meet him at the rendezvous point after 10 miles of freeway where he hands Dane the rental's keys and a canister lifted from a drive-through bank.

"All right, my wife's gonna grill you. You've got to be cool. You're a treetop flyer, all right?

"Yeah, I've got this."

"You really didn't bring anything back? I know Sunday brought something back from Mexico."

"No, ma'am. You know I don't lie to you."

"I don't believe you. I don't want you endangering my son. I don't want any of that kind of shit here."

"Sunday took it all with him. It's all in his truck."

"All right, that's pretty good, Pops. What if you get pulled over?"

"Well, Sunday, I don't have a license."

“Yeah, but what are you going to say? All right, I’m the cop.”

“Ain’t no cop’s gonna pull me over, Sunday. I’m just gonna drive the speed limit the whole way, and baby girl gave me all the directions.”

“That’s good, Pops, but what do you say to the cop? License and registration.”

“Yes sir. Let me see, sir. Well, see, this is a rental car, and here’s the registration.”

“Where’s your license?”

“Right, yes. It’s here in my wallet. Just a second. Then, I’m gonna rummage around in my pockets a bit, yeah? Man, it was here, somewhere, I’m sure.”

“Where you headed?”

“I’m just going down to Ogden to see my daughter. She rented this car for me so I could come visit. She’s in college, and she doesn’t get much time off anymore.”

“We’re going to have to search the car. Get out of the car.”

"Do you really want me to get out of the car?"

"No, just, I'm still the cop, all right?"

"Oh, right, right. Okay, sir, I'll get out of the car. That's fine. He's not gonna find it, right, Sunday?"

"No, he wouldn't find it. It's double duct-taped and sealed and sealed again. Not even a dog could find it. Look, Pops, you know you don't have to do this. I mean, I don't want my baby girl to get in trouble, so I could throw it out in this parking lot right here, hundreds of dollars of this stuff, pills and everything. I'd make some homeless junkie real happy."

"Oh, no, no, Sunday. I'm a treetop flier! Born survivor!"

"All right. But just remember, it's your choice, okay?"

"Yeah, I know. I'm gonna do it. You can count on me."

"All right, just try not to talk too much, Pops. They'll know you're nervous."

"Okay, Sunday, but I'm just gonna drive the speed limit."

"Not too far under, and not too far over."

"Not too far under, not too far over."

They eliminated the ability to possess language, abandoned the notions of who said or wrote what until they spoke as a two-mouthed monster, its simultaneous speech a din beyond language.

After breakfast with King David the homeless man, Dad drives everyone to Walmart to clean out the truck. I scrunch my nose at a moldy Subway sandwich in the backseat.

“This is what I’ve been talking about. You come around here with all your fucked-up feminine energy wearing exactly the face my wife gets, and you have all these expectations. Get that fucking energy out of here! You can’t even go a full day without some bitchy expression on your face!” he says.

“You know what? Fine,” I say as I grab my satchel and plastic Walmart bag out of the front seat. “Checkout’s at three. You left cash on the nightstand.”

He calls after me, “You can wander off, but you can’t fucking leave!”

In the coffee shop that gives me reprieve, I say, "Sometimes I feel like my timeline folded over itself. It's as if my timeline reversed and now I'm looking back from the past at my future."

"That's what it looks like in the fifth dimension," Eve says.

I stare out the window of an Airbnb Eve and I rent on the Oregon coast and let my eyes go out of focus. The white space between the trees moves high above the ground, teasing me with human shapes. A man with a stroller. A small child with pigtails. When I refocus my eyes, they are gone.

The two of us walk across the street to the cold Pacific shoreline and approach the ocean. I feel the summons in the sand. The sun is beginning to set on the watery horizon in a style typical of the Pacific Northwest, not with blasts the colors of dying leaves but with gradations of blue and gray lined into the cloud cover as though it were dawn and not twilight.

We walk along a small freshwater tributary as it drains toward its saltwater counterpart. As the tributary nears the waves, they mix, the ocean widening the tributary and breaking its banks slightly each time waves crash on the shore. Even small movements of the waves have an effect on the momentum of the tributary in ripples like a language we can't read. I add more ripples with my feet as I walk through the water.

I walk further into the ocean, though both pairs of our jeans soak in the saltwater. Still, the summons, the draw, remains. I find myself unwilling to stop walking in. I want to walk and walk and dissolve into the being god that is the ocean.

But, I do turn around after my thighs brush with the ocean's liquid hands, and the world begins again. Someone has written "A + E" in the sand, though there is no one else on the beach.

When the two of us walk back, I see a bookstore with the cockpit of a plane attached and wonder how it got there. I was sure there used to be a garden here, but there is only parking lot. I see a dumpster that announces "CARDBOARD ONLY." I throw the old world in there and keep walking.

"If I'm being honest, I want us both to crack under the weight of this intensity. I want us to pour out and fill each other up in ways we have never overflowed because we have confidence in what we are. I want to taste what oozes out of you when you crack and break reality with our own disbelief in it."

∞

Dad

Today 3:43 PM

Wherever and whatever you are, I can cross realms as well, but I believe your heart has been stained so badly by the truth, lies, and in between that YOU still can't believe whom your King is and will be till he dies . . . Right when God lets me swim the realms without this body till I get bored.

Ask reality to let those teeth-yellow scales fall from your eyes, my Princess—your King will fail you in terms of earth time all the time, but I will never fail you—I simply love you too much to ever let that happen again—

Graduation, that shit was yesterday.

I have apologized, Forgiveness is the treasure not of the hearers, but of the Listeners. Those fucking scales are falsely forcing a worn-out narrative over top of reality and keeping you from sharing richly in this experience.

Today 4:01 PM

Processing doesn't happen instantaneously, Dad.

Go back to the hotel without me. We can figure it out later.

“So, if the multiverse theory is correct, then each possibility plays out in some other reality. So, maybe the ‘video-game’ feeling is what happens when one version of yourself dies somewhere and your consciousness travels to a place where your awareness continues. And maybe, from your own perspective, you live out your life to the last possible moment when you could still be alive in any of those places.”

“You know, this kind of sounds like the quantum immortality argument,” Eve says.

“What?”

“It’s also called quantum suicide. Say you are in a room with a bomb, and the bomb has a 50 percent chance of going off when you press the detonate button. Assuming it is truly random, it is logical to think that you have a 50 percent chance of dying, right? Well, you press the button once, and you don’t die. You press the button a second time, and you still don’t die. You press the button three, four, five, ten, a hundred times. You still aren’t dead. Why?”

“Because you wouldn’t know if you were dead?”

“Every time you press the button, you split the universe in two: one where you died and one where you didn’t die. But because consciousness *is* awareness and you can’t really be aware of death, you will always continue living as long as there is any possibility where you could still be alive.”

“But lots of people commit suicide and succeed.”

“You just happen to live in one of the universes where they succeeded. From their own perspective somewhere else, they survived.”

Our brain is not a "stand alone" information processing organ

the brain is conceived *in a holographic* *field*

resonant

meta-stable

communicating

as a

multi-cavity network

in a non-dual manner

updating a time-symmetric global memory space

conceived as operating from a

(hyper-sphere)

consciousness

in the entire universe

coupling

model of *self*

and algorithmic origin

"I don't want to leave here. I want to leave a piece of myself, but if I keep dividing myself, there will be nothing left of me."

"You cannot take away from yourself. You can only add. You will be no less whole by leaving a piece of yourself here. And besides, I'll make you a trade. A piece of me for a piece of you."

"What does 343 mean to you?"

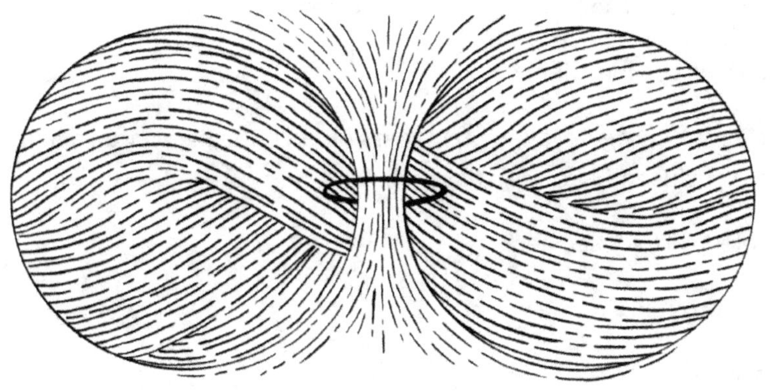

"Want to just start at the beginning?" the university therapist asks.

"I keep . . . well, I keep seeing this woman."

"Is this woman real?"

"No, I don't think so. No one else can see her."

"What does she look like?"

"She's about my age. Maybe a few years older. Long, light brown hair. She's translucent, like she's barely there."

"How often do you see her?"

"Maybe a couple times a week?"

"Does she speak?"

"Sometimes we have conversations."

"Does she have a name?"

"Eve."

∞

"There's only a 20 percent chance that I'm sane," I tell Eve.

"How do you figure?"

"Well, I'm a poet, and 30 percent of writers go insane. Plus my dad has Bipolar I with psychotic delusions, and that's genetic, so there's another 50 percent."

"That's not how statistics work."

"Your dad is going to play a song at the funeral, and F is doing the program design. I thought it would be nice if you wrote a poem about your brother and read it. So we don't have to use something generic. We could put it on the back of the program."

"The funeral, it's in a week, right?" I ask.

"If you can't do it, that's all right. I just thought you might want to."

"I'll think about it."

There were eight large hospitals in municipal Salt Lake City.
I could count them on my fingers:
LDS, St. Marks, University, Regional . . .

My baby brother died in a hospital. Half-awake, half-alive, he
never cried; the world never gave him reason.

An old couple ask me for directions
though they are closer to one hospital than the other.
Pointing west, I ask, "Who's dying?"

I was at home when he died. I didn't watch my parents hold him
while the life support dwindled.

"We want to make everyone comfortable . . ."
Fifty seven percent of deaths occur in hospitals,
and, still, the nurse has to explain to me:
". . . family members die here."

If H has two cups of grief and Dad has three, how many are left
when Dad leaves?

My brother lives here.
He lives in the apartment next door
where a child cries in darkness.

Can you grieve for someone after knowing them for three days?

I lost Dad when he punched a hole in the wall, but the maintenance
crew patched it 12 minutes later.

My brother lives in the smell of the hospitals I visit.
He lives in his own absence.

There are new hospitals now that I've left; I don't know
this city. It's as unrecognizable as my family
post-mortem.

∞

“I want to be a body of words,” I tell Eve.

“That’d be a neat Halloween costume.”

“I don’t want to wait that long.”

∞

"Do you think it's okay to cut this quote short?"

"You're the artists."

"Should we include the quotation marks?"

"You're the artists."

"Stop crying. You'll smear the ink."

"Crying is always happening."

"I'm writing that on your nose."

Everything has been called into question. Even in the best of times the daily world is tenuous to her, a thin iridescent skin held in place by surface tension. She puts a lot of effort into keeping it together, her willed illusion of comfort and stability, the words flowing from left to right, the routines of love; but underneath is darkness. Menace, chaos, cities aflame, towers crashing down, the anarchy of deep water. Eve writes in black pen across and around the meat of my thigh.

"He sent me another picture."

"Another one? What is that, like, 30 now?"

"Something like that."

"Let me see," Eve says. "That's a lot of weed."

"How much do you think he spent?"

"You think he *bought* it all? What's there, a full pound?"

"Why's he flipping it off? Or is he flipping the camera off?"

"At least his teeth look nice."

∞

"I'm not in a good way, sweetheart, but I need company."

"Do you want me to come now?"

"Yes. When you get here, we can go see the fish."

"Do you need me to stop and grab anything?"

"Two packs of Marlboro 100s."

"Should I bring—"

"No, come alone. I don't want anyone else to see me like this.
Just come up here, and we'll go see the fish. I want to see the fish."

[footsteps going up and downstairs]

John: Let's start again. For the whole congregation!

[muffled guitar and sax sounds]

∞

"WHY WON'T ANYBODY HELP ME? Am I so much of a bad guy?"

"We *are* . . . We are trying to help."

"Then take me to the goddamned hospital."

"If I don't make it through this, you have to write the book, Kassandra. I have some money saved away for you—no one even knows about it—just promise me . . ."

∞

"I must really be going crazy because it seems like there are actually words on your face," he says.

"Tell me a happy story about John. There has to be one."

It’s a wonder anyone can live in the house
where Dad taught me to build fires.

There, sprawled near the fireplace, I pushed
my bare toes close to flames and read

what my mother hadn’t screened yet.
I slept with the vent

to fill my blanket with warmth,
and when the heater turned off, Dad danced

to bring it back. Rituals are easier with thermostats.
I waited for him in that pea-green living room, waited

while dinner grew cold and my sister fell
asleep in her spaghetti. When my father walked

through the door and headed to the garage, I memorized
the songs he sang.

Dad banished spirits from me beside that fireplace;
when I sneezed them away, the spirits melted

into the walls of the house to watch,
air choked with the gravity of memory.

But, in my dreams, it is that house I defend
when Ben Lomond becomes a volcano,

when doors refuse to lock, when the daughter
I don't have falls off the deck Dad built.

I finger-painted that deck once. My friends told me
no one would notice.

Dad made me sand the paint away,
though it would have been easier to burn it.

∞

"I have to go back to Mexico, Kassandra. They're the only ones who can fix this tooth."

"¿Entiendes, mi hermana?"

my own fucking daughter

can’t

I touch my own ?

I touch my own daughter

my own fucking daughter

my own daughter?

I can’t fucking

touch

my

daughter?

can’t own
my

touch fucking daughter

I own

my fucking daughter

can’t touch

I fucking
own
my daughter

∞

"I have no more voice," he tells them.

"Then just play that good ol' guitar."

“. . . these goons you’re working for now, they’re not working from experience in the industry. They want to be all buddy-buddy, but people like you and me, we just want to be real. We’d call it ‘Konecny-Gomez Lumber,’ and we could hold all our meetings in bars, shit, what with all the clients we’ll have. Besides, my employees make 40 percent commissions,” he says.

There is a full centimeter of white around the perimeter of his irises. He tilts his large head and raises his eyebrows to look older than he is.

“You know, I go down to Los Algodones, and everyone knows me there! They even gave me a nickname. I’m not another fuckin’ gringo to them, you know? They don’t try to sell shit to me. They know I’m not a tourist. I might be white, but I’m Mexican on the inside,” he says to persuade the lumber broker.

“You can’t make this shit up,” he says.

Either everything is fiction or nothing is.

"What'll it be, Sunday?"

∞

Dad asks God to choose songs from his phone on the way to John Day. Apparently, God uses my dad's finger to scroll and touch one at random.

"Maybe MAGI is an acronym. Make America Great, I," he says with reverence. "Holy shit. Make America Great, I. That's what I named my band. And I'm gonna play at the bar in John Day. John Day, the town where my first baby girl was born."

I remain silent.

"That's right! That's right! Fuck you, God! Fuck you. I never asked for this."

God forgets to choose the next song, and a recording begins to play through the aux cable.

Sunday: Hold on a second, one. Okay. Do you still like me?

King David: Oh yes.

Sunday: Okay, then would you...You don't have to do anything for me for what I did for you, but if you would, just for other people to understand how God's love works, would you just tell the story? You can make it crazy, you can cuss, you can do whatever. God loves you...

King David (interrupting): Oh yes, he does.

Sunday: ...and God sent me to you specifically today to tell you that. And now I'm going to walk away from the truck, just talk into the phone if you would. If you don't want to... I'll hit the... I'll turn it off. Would you mind? Thank you. Talk as long as you want, explain your story, do whatever, but tell how you first met...

King David (interrupting): All right.

Sunday (continuing): ...me, Domingo.

King David: All right, I first met Domingo at... came into Pendleton, Oregon here at the Walmart. I was hitchhiking from the Tri City, Washington on my way to Utah to be with my wife who was locked up. Because of a five-year-old warrant.

Sunday: For what? I'm... I'm still lighting my cigarette. For what?

King David: For possession of... simple possession of meth...

Sunday (interrupting): Was she dealing...

King David (interrupting): No.

Sunday (continuing): ...1,000 pounds of meth?

King David: No, she was sitting in a hotel room with a bunch of friends...

Sunday (interrupting): Was she clean when she got arrested?!

King David: She was...

Sunday (interrupting): Mostly?

King David: She was just high. Didn't have anything else, just high.

Sunday (distantly): Yeah, "just high" is not dirty. It's not dirty, bro. It's a plant. I'm a supporter of the plant!

King David (louder now, closer to the phone): And they searched the room and found a little baggy and no one would cop to it, and my wife's name was on the room, so they gave the charge to her.

Sunday (overlapping): Oh yes, America! You're winning the fucking War on Drugs, aren't you?! Now tell the story, King David!

King David: So, outside... standing outside of Taco Bell at Walmart, flying a sign trying to get some money to get towards Utah. Domingo pulls up... um... screeches to a halt right on the wrong side of the road right by me by the stop sign and tells me God sent him to me to tell me that I'm doing, um, right, and he bless… blesses me so much. He's been a godsend. He has a very good blessing. And now he's helping me to get to, um, to my wife. And feeling very blessed. God is good. God is very good. Amen. And I also got to say that, um, that I'm very blessed to meet the...both of them. And God is very good. Yes, God is so good and he will, um, watch over me and see me through all that I'm going through to get my wife and see that she gets through this and get back...back to where we need to be. Yes. God is good. Thank you, Lord. Amen.

“And now we’re going back to the manger! We’re going back to the manger where my baby girl was born.”

∞

Sunday: When I... This is (laughter)... This is Magi 1. When I had the urge to make a statement by roaring up to David in the beautiful truck that God's blessed me with and my beautiful life that God's blessed me with and my beautiful wife that God's blessed me with, I had no idea... No idea... oh mi poor amor, no (indistinct attempts at Spanish in a tearful voice).

(Voice returns to normal) Both of our little niños are playing together on God's playground in the realms. Together. For love. And... and King David, uh, this is seven hours after his speech of double-barreled prayer badass shit. He's gotta message 'cause we're about ready to part company and we've had a great day, haven't we David?

King David: Oh yes. Oh, Lord.

Sunday: Okay. King David's gonna take over. Praise the Lord for the whole congregation!

King David: Oh yes.

Sunday (distantly): Headed to the Motel 6, right?

King David: Yep. Headed to the Motel 6. Well, when I... when I was younger, I was have... having a father-son day. He was five years old, and yeah, at that time, I was in the game, selling and doing all different kind of drugs, drinking, and everything. Anything I could get my hands on I could make a buck.

Sunday: Right.

King David: And I didn't...

Sunday: You weren't...Were you a treetop flier?

King David: Oh yeah.

Sunday: Yeah! Born survivor!

King David: And I didn't...um...

Sunday (distantly): And we hurt the people around us.

King David: And I didn't... Yeah, I was just about to say I didn't care what toes I stepped on to get what I wanted.

Sunday: I've been that guy certain times in my life.

King David: And unfortunately... um, one, uh, Father's Day, I was having a father-son day, a little window shopping with my boy, when someone was at... took an attempt on my life, trying to take me out of competition, but instead of gettin' me, the bullet went through my hip and went into my son, and my son ended up dying in my arms five minutes later.

(long pause)

Sunday: How do guys like us who've had those tremendous kind of losses still love God so much? In your... I mean, just your opinion, King David.

∞

King David: Well, I'm a strong believer, um, everything happens for a reason...in God's time, not ours.

Sunday (interrupting): Not our time.

King David: In God's time.

Sunday: He's the boss. We're never the boss.

King David: And even though, um, people think I'm weird, but like, I tell people, it's like, even though everybody knows the Devil, Lucifer…

Sunday: Diablo!

King David: Even... even him! Even though...

Sunday: I'm God's little devil. I'm God's Diablo!

King David: The light's green.

Sunday (laughing): "The light's green."

King David: And even though he's the devil, in technicality, he's still of God because he's a fallen angel.

Sunday: Yeah, he's a fallen angel. I'm just a naughty angel.

"Remember when God told Abraham to sacrifice Isaac, Kassandra? He really thought he was going to have to sacrifice his son. And, he would have done it, too, just because God asked him to. That's the important bit. If God hadn't intervened . . . he would have done it. He would have done it. He would have killed his son, his baby," John says. "We're going back to the manger. The manger where my baby girl was born. I'm taking you back to the manger."

He puts his hand on my thigh.

Sunday: There's only two real rules: He's the boss and do unto others as you would have them do onto you. Those are the only two real rules.

King David: Yep.

Sunday: Jesus didn't die on a cross, he died on a pole! He died on a tree! They didn't waste an extra nail on Jesus!

King David: Huh?

Sunday: He was... he was a pain in the government's ass, and they were not going to waste... He didn't start Christianity; Christianity hadn't started yet! He was a fucking revolutionary, and that's my Jesus and I love him and he fucking loves me, too. He's my brother.

King David: Exactly right.

Sunday: And he's your fucking brother, too, bro.

King David: Yep.

Sunday: And we can't do no wrong. As long as we... as long as we're praising Jesus while we're being naughty, there's nothing we can do wrong. And that... that sucks for people who don't get that. Go ahead, I don't want to take up any more of your time.

King David: Oh, I’m done, brother.

Sunday: You’re done? I’m done, too.

King David: Amen, brother.

Sunday: Amen, for the whole congregation, right? All the MAGI?

King David: Huh?

Sunday: Say “all the MAGI.”

King David: For all the MAGI.

(Sunday’s laughter)

Sunday: All of ‘em.

King David: All of ‘em.

Sunday: We’re all brothers and sisters, bro. Hit the button, man. Hit the button.

"Fuck you, God! I didn't ask for this. I didn't ask to be famous. We're going back to the manger. I'm taking my baby girl back to the manger! Fuck you, God!"

King David: And even though, um, people think I'm weird, but like, I tell people, it's like, even though everybody knows the Devil, Lucifer...

Sunday: Diablo!

King David: Even... even him! Even though...

Sunday: I'm God's little devil. I'm God's Diablo!

On a short straightaway of the narrow, snow-blanketed road, he speeds up to 50, 60 miles per hour, the four-wheel drive grating in my ears as the truck hugs curves at double the speed limit.

Sunday (overlapping): Oh yes, America! You’re winning the fucking War on Drugs, aren’t you?!

He pulls his hand off my leg, but I keep my body still and my voice silent.

King David: Even... even him! Even though...

Sunday: I'm God's little devil. I'm God's Diablo!

King David: Oh, I'm done, brother.

Sunday: You're done? I'm done, too.

King David: Amen, brother.

Sunday: Amen, for the whole congregation, right? All the MAGI?

King David: Huh?

Sunday: Say "all the MAGI."

King David: For all the MAGI.

(Sunday's laughter)

When he reaches to clasp his fingers around my left arm, I scream. I scream Eve's name. I scream and scream and cannot stop screaming.

∞

"Do you think less of me now that you know where I break?" I ask Eve.

"Strength isn't about your breaking point. It's about how you handle yourself when you're broken."

∞

The hotel manager tells me I am beautiful
with yesterday's curls
when I sneak around the pool enclosure
to avoid my dad.
I feel naked in my bright orange sweater

that does nothing for the cold in my body.
Later, I'll tell my dad God wanted me to leave
so he'll listen, but now I walk past the Thriftway
where my mom begged him for my first dog. Past
the Chevron, a woman shouts, "I bet

it was a man, wasn't it?"
Along the creek my infant body swam in,
I cross the street
where my dad tied my bottle to a fishing pole.
Maybe I have always been so gullible.

I escape in a U-Haul
because there is nothing else,
a 10-foot void for locked doors
and a driver's seat.
Between towns that share my parents' names,

I still scream out for life
on a snow-covered highway.

The great secret known to Apollonius of Tyana, John of Tarsus, Simon Magus, Asklepios, Paracelsus, Boehme and Bruno is that: we are moving backward in time. The universe in fact is contracting into a unitary entity which is completing itself. Decay and disorder are seen by us in reverse, as increasing. These healers learned to move forward in time, which is retrograde to us.

"I can't do it," I say out loud after waking at three in the morning. "I'm done, and he was right. I did know how to end it. I do know how. I don't want this pain anymore. I'm ready for it to be over. Either I die here and let my consciousness go altogether, or it has to get better because I can't keep living like this."

I whisper my last words to Eve and let everything sink into darkness.

∞

It's dark, and I am pulling Eve along to the seaside. I watch the waves burst against the rocky shore like nature's aneurysms.

I think, *I am the wind, and you, the waves.* Eve's voice beside my ear is a vacuum of sound when Eve asks me to come back. The surf reflects only the stars. Later, I hand over the hotel keycard, the air between us now charged with the burgeoning storm's lightning, and I can't help but kiss Eve once the door closes.

When I am naked on the bed and Eve kisses the length of my body, there is something magnetic about Eve's skin. It has a gravity over me. When Eve inserts a finger inside me, the inner parts of me open up, and suddenly I know why so many euphemisms about the vulva have to do with flowering. When I put my mouth to Eve's opening and allow Eve to reciprocate, an intoxicating flow of energy surges into my mouth from Eve and back again after traveling the length of us. I forget the boundaries of self. I have never shared essence so completely. Images of black-and-white circles in varying sizes burst into my mind, and I imagine painting them. Later, I'll spend eight hours getting the texture right.

After we both finish, we do not speak. I hold Eve until she falls asleep and later get up from bed to take pictures of my naked body. I want to remember exactly what I look like.

∞

When I shower, the synesthesia lingers. Looking at the decoratively warped bathroom window, the rays of light appear like undulating jellyfish tentacles, and when I get into the water, I run my hand over the streams as though they are harp strings.

A voice I don't recognize asks, "Do you want an idea or a baby?"

Two weeks later, I tie my tubes.

∞

"You know how, if you look at the universe at a large enough scale, it starts to look like atoms?"

"Yeah," Eve says.

"Well, it seems like there might not be anything that happens on a small scale that doesn't also happen on a large scale. Put differently, I don't think there is anything that happens to an individual that does not also happen to a system as a whole."

"I feel like there are flaws in that argument."

"Well, sure, but assume that it's true for a second."

"Okay."

"If that's true and the quantum immortality argument is also true, then that would mean that humanity or consciousness or the universe itself also has quantum immortality. The possibilities would always split to preserve the universe where the universe could still be aware of itself."

"So, in other words, you're saying that, because the universe somehow created self-awareness, it is no longer possible for the world as a whole to die?"

"Yes! We've had the capacity to destroy the planet for half a century now. Why did we choose now to suddenly start being rational and diplomatic?"

"Mutually assured destruction? Social evolution?"

"Maybe the world did end. Maybe the world is always ending. But consciousness continues in the one where it didn't. Where there was a ceasefire. Where diplomacy worked. If we can consider quantum immortality on an individual level, we can also consider it on a planetary scale. The microcosm reflects into the macrocosm and vice versa."

Dad

Today 8:32 PM

<message type="SMS">
<address>xxxxxx8372</address>
<body>PS+you+didn%27t+run+from+me+in+Joh
n+day%2C+you+ran+from+yourself.%0AMaybe+
go+back+by+yourself+and+face+what+you+clea
rly+were+not+ready+to.</body>
<date>1488414319565</date>
<read>1</read>
<type>1</type>
</message>

“I still hear those recordings play in my head sometimes.”

Dad

Today 6:23 AM

I'll give you five grand to come with me to Mexico

I already hooked Pops up with a beautiful
50-year-old massage therapist named Rose—
you can't make this shit up!

I'll give you five grand to come with me to Mexico

Need a pretty girl

Today 11:55 AM

Can't without a pretty girl
I am that desperate for human attention

Today 4:02 PM

Lonely

Lonely

Lonely

Lonely

Lonely

Lonely

Lonely

Lonely

Please leave me alone I am so lonely

Love, beyond providing emotional sustenance, compassion, and companionship, is now expected to act as a panacea for existential aloneness as well

We turn to one person for the protection and emotional connections that a multitude of social networks used to provide.

I allow a spirit healer to analyze the damage Dad left. The healer runs his hands over my left arm and tells me someone has barbs in me there. I follow the traces of the barbs back to their source and find it in my past when I am a child and someone tugs on my wrist abruptly. As the healer picks the barbs out, I gain more feeling in my arm.

The healer scans my body for other harm and settles around my solar plexus. The harm buried there feels the healer's gaze and retreats deeper inside me. I follow the red substance as it melts into the texture of taffy and falls into the core of me, hitting an old fallen tree trunk with wrinkled bark. When the red substance hits the wood, it ignites a section into live coals.

As though performing surgery, the healer takes each ember out piecemeal as if removing a ruptured cyst.

The healer then moves upward to the space between my breasts in his scan, but I say, "No, that's mine. I know what lives there."

∞

"Look, you can't tell anybody, but I'm going to the hearing tomorrow. I'm driving and I've got Pops in the car, and we're going to take back my boy. His mom needs a break. She needs to get clean. I'm going to take him to Mexico."

"Wait, wait, what do you mean, 'get clean'?"

"Kassandra, you have to have noticed that she's on drugs. They all say *I* need a drug test, but look at her! How come nobody drug tests her? She's probably on meth or prescription pills, which are worse than meth! I'm going to take my boy to Mexico."

"Why do you think she's on drugs?"

"She takes so many pills! The pills make her crazy! You can't parent while you're crazy on pills like that."

"Dad, I don't think she's abusing any drugs."

"Well, I'm going to tell the court she needs a drug test. And I'm taking my boy to Mexico."

I twist my hair into a tight bun and wear heavy eyeshadow like war paint. My lips are a bright red gash against the sleepless pallor of my face. I drive 15 hours through the night to be at the protective order hearing.

"The plaintiff would like to call Kassandra Lighthouse to the witness stand."

"Please state your full name into the microphone."

"Do you swear that the evidence you shall give shall be the truth, the whole truth, and nothing but the truth, so help you God?"

"Did your father call you yesterday?"

"What was the nature of that phone call?"

"While you were on the phone with him, did he threaten anyone?"

"It didn't happen like that," Dad interjects.

I count the stones on my grandmother's old wedding ring.
The ring rotates around and around on my thumb.

One, two, three, four, five, six, seven. Seven, six.

"Objection, your Honor."

"Sustained."

"Do you have reason to believe that the respondent would harm his wife or their son?"

“What leads you to believe that?”

six

five

four

three

“Does your father have a history of taking illegal drugs?”

two one one two three

“Which ones?”

“I’m clean. *You* take a piss test. *You* do a mental evaluation. They already let me out twice!”

seven

six five

“Objection, your Honor.”

“Sustained.”

four six seven
seven
seven

"Have you spent time with your father recently?"

"And why did you stop travelling with him?"

"How did you get away from your father?"

"Does the respondent have any questions for the witness?"
four two three

one

Dad looks at the judge and shakes his head.

There is a family of deer outside the courthouse.

"That's what real love looks like, huh, Mom?"

“We’ve had an agricultural revolution and an industrial revolution, and now it’s time we have a spiritual revolution, or we aren’t going to be able to cope with how quickly our world keeps changing.”

“Are you talking about a new religion?”

“I don’t think so. I’m talking about communication. I’m talking about a revolution of meaning and time. I think it’s already happening.”

"I wonder when your compassion for him will run out."

"If someone had a brain tumor that made them act this way, would you blame them? Would it be their fault? No. I don't have any evidence to say it's any different with my dad."

Language has made us more than a group of pack-hunting monkeys; it's made us a group of pack-hunting monkeys with a dream. And the fallout from that dream has given us our glory and our shame. Our weaponry, our technology, our art, our hopes, our fears. All of this arises out of our own ability to articulate and communicate with each other. And I use this in the broad sense. I mean, for me, the glory of the human animal is cognitive activity. Song, dance, sculpture, poetry—all of these cognitive activities—when we participate in them, we cross out of the domain of animal organization and into the domain of a genuine relationship to the transcendent.

I am in my living room. Eve is asleep on the couch, but I am just lying there, staring at the popcorn ceiling. Though I can still see the ceiling, another image superimposes itself there, not completely inside my mind, not completely outside it. There is an expanse of darkness with only a thin disc of prismatic color in my view. The disc suddenly grows wider and changes patterns as it blurs the edges of where the disc meets darkness. As this process continues, the disc begins to move upward, leaving solid afterimages of itself and creating a funnel. I notice that the outside of the funnel has lines to illustrate its curvature.

The funnel reaches a point where it cannot widen out any further in the darkness, so rather than change its momentum, the funnel folds out over itself as if it were a fountain of color.

I suddenly realize that this new fountain shape is not unidirectional. In viewing it from the opening at the top, I feel the possibility of moving downward but also know that doing so would force the entire possibility to collapse. While I continue looking, and thereby moving in a spiraling drill pattern downward into the fountain, the edges begin to decay as if I am staring down the center of a wilting plant. To return to the healthy fountain, I simply look up, and the prismatic colors return. It is only a matter of perspective.

Outside the fountain again, I watch as the whole thing becomes smaller and smaller until I am in the next dimension. The fountain has condensed into a single point of prismatic color, and as I reach to touch it, the movements of my hands draw more of them on the ceiling. I am drawing with the blueprints of the universe itself.

"If you think about time as a straight horizontal line going off into infinity, then I imagine that my line looks something a little more like a skinny sine wave. I just fit more in the same space that everyone calls time. Except, maybe time isn't linear at all and this is all some kind of overlapping spiral."

“I feel crazy. Like, totally insane. Who has visions like that on marijuana? I didn’t even have that much.”

“You’ve told me that mushrooms just prevent you from blocking out nonstandard reality. Maybe you just need an inhibitor sometimes. Edibles and mushrooms seem to have the same effect on you.”

“Do you think I’m losing it? Like my dad?” I ask.

“No. John isolated himself. He’s removed the context that makes it possible for most people to understand him. He refuses to explain. He’s burned the bridges and cut ties and stands alone. You, on the other hand, have the capacity to provide context. You fold people into your ideas. You create bridges. You’re the scientist who regularly comes away from the microscope.”

“Isn’t that an Alan Watts quote?”

“Maybe,” Eve says, grinning.

“Insanity as the inability to provide context. I like that definition.”

“Me too. You want to know something?”

“What?”

“I believe you.”

"I want to stay with you. I know that I could exist without you, but I don't want to."

"I think our timelines are joined together. Or if they're not . . . I can see them."

"What do you mean?"

"I could pull them together. Would you like me to?"

"Our entire timelines? How?"

"I've traveled in the fifth dimension. I traveled here to find you, didn't I?"

"Yes."

"You know that the fourth dimension is time. So, objects traveling in the fourth dimension look like long, skinny worms. They're full timelines. The fifth dimension is possibility. You can see cross sections of time, which is the fourth dimension, so I can see cross sections of the sixth dimension. I can fold them through."

"But why me?"

"Because I love you. I've always loved you. I will always love you. You called, and I answered. I've looked for you for a long time. But you still have this choice. Would you like me to pull our timelines together?"

"I would like that," I say.

"There. It is done."

∞

. . . brings,
brings, thus, the
poem
for-
wards (of which I
am mere-
ly its
in-

stance: pre-
fix for setting
sub-
stance to

syllable.   for
bringing the
un-
worked images: *damp*
bulb, plump
fire, for-
wards, into their
linked

and sonorous be-
trothals).

“What’s 343 mean to you?”

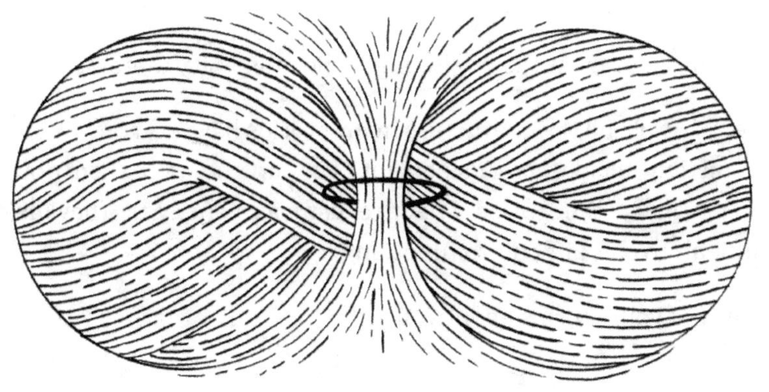

"Want to just start at the beginning?" the university therapist asks.

"I keep . . . well, all the characters in my stories have started committing suicide. I can't sleep until I get up and write them down. I can't even use the stories. They are just fragments. But, they make it difficult to eat, difficult to function."

"Are any of your stories about yourself?"

"There's only a 20 percent chance that I'm sane," I tell Eve on our second date.

"How do you figure?"

"Well, I'm a poet, and 30 percent of writers go insane. Plus my dad has Bipolar I with psychotic delusions, and that's genetic, so there's another 50 percent."

"That's not how statistics work."

∞

"Your dad is going to play a song at the funeral, and F is doing the program design. I thought it would be nice if you wrote a poem about your brother and read it. So we don't have to use something generic. We could put it on the back of the program."

"The funeral, it's in a week, right?" I ask.

"How's she doing? Kassandra, I mean," he asks.

"She's managing. Still processing everything."

"I can't tell if she's growing or getting smaller. It's like she's on the other side of this opaque glass, and I can't tell whether she's shrinking or just moving away from me."

"I think she's getting bigger," Eve says. He nods as he blows smoke out of his mouth.

"I can see why you love her. She wakes up the dragons in people."

"I'm very lucky to have met her." He nods again, and they stand awkwardly in silence.

"And you, what do you think of me?" He asks.

"I don't think you're as dangerous they say you are."

"That's probably true. I'm tired, though. I'm so tired. Do you know what it's like to have your kid die? I suppose you wouldn't, would you. It kills something inside you. Something inside your own body breaks. My baby boy. Kassandra told you, right? Trisomy 18. He died in my arms three days after he was born. My little niño. Held him while they took him off life support."

"She said you punched a hole in the hospital wall."

"I did. They patched it right quick. Like it was never there at all."

"Makes you feel like you can't make an impression on the world."

"I can, though. You know I can. I have. Look at Kassandra."

"It's one way to get her where she's going. But she would be going there anyway, John."

"I think you're right. But I can't stop this. It's already happening. I know what I am."

"The path may be fixed, but identity isn't. You cut yourself off when you know who you are."

"From the voices? From God?"

"From whatever you want to call it."

∞

On the way to Newport, I sing:

Up on Cripple Creek, she sends me
If I spring a leak, she mends me
I don't have to speak, she defends me
A drunkard's dream if I ever did see one

The song sounds wrong every time I get to "drunkard's dream." Dad could never get those chords right. How many times had I heard him repeat that as a kid?

John: *I never meant to cause you any sorrow. Never meant to cause you any pain...*

“She’s not going to help me. Nobody’s helping me. I think I need to go to the emergency room.”

“Let’s see if we can get you an appointment first.”

“WHY WON’T ANYBODY HELP ME? Am I so much of a bad guy?”

“We *are* . . . We are trying to help.”

“Then take me to the goddamned hospital.”

"He'll need to take these antibiotics twice daily, and we've prescribed him some high-dose ibuprofen since you requested that we not give him any opiates. Don't let him take more than four of these a day. And keep him from drinking. He'll need to take this one on an empty stomach and take this one after he's eaten something. Can you sign . . ."

“If I don’t make it through this, you have to write the book, Kassandra. I have some money saved away for you—no one even knows about it—just promise me . . . ”

Once Eve leaves, he says, “If someone had looked at me that way, maybe I wouldn’t have gotten divorced.”

∞

Eve hasn't heard from me, but I left Newport more than four hours ago. Eve looks out the window compulsively and sees the fog. *She's afraid of it,* Eve remembers. The doorknob rattles; Eve hears someone struggling with the stubborn key. Opening it for me, I collapse inside just past the reach of the door.

"I'm sorry. I'm sorry," I say.

"What's wrong? What happened?"

"I'm sorry. I'm sorry. I'msorryI'msorryI'msorry . . ."

"Did you crash the car?"

". . . I'msorryI'msorryI'msorry . . ."

"Are you apologizing to me or to yourself?"

"I don't pretend to know."

∞

“Tell me a happy story about John. There has to be one.”

“There were. There are. There’s, well . . .

∞

My parents fell in love
over the phone. They talked for months

before meeting in person. She brought
a stuffed bear and arrived early

to the bed and breakfast.
He had long hair then, curly

and dark chocolate brown.
They met halfway and walked over

a trestle bridge. My mother, a jolly
blonde giant with doe legs, didn't trip

when a train chased them off and disappeared.
My parents had the same memory, described

the ghost train with identical detail,
memories not erased after post-adrenaline sleep.

Somehow, she hadn't fallen through the slats.
Maybe it was the same train

∞

I saw on the motorcycle with Dad at 11.
We had only one set of clothes

and swimsuits. Maybe he and I fell asleep
on the same rock counting train cars

we later passed on the road.

Maybe they really died that day.

Maybe I was never born and he never told me
to write the book. In that alternate reality,

the train crashed early, and the planes
never left the ground.

∞

"I just . . . this whole situation . . . I've had to rely on you so much. Aren't you getting tired of me? Of this? How much is too much?"

"Kassandra, I came here knowing fully well that not everything that happened to us was going to be easy. But, I love you. I came here for you."

"I just want to stay in bed all day."

"Didn't R tell you, back before things really blew up, that he thought John's relationships would get better if he just sat down and watched some Netflix?"

"Yeah," I laugh, "it's a lot better than throwing plates."

In an announcer voice, Eve says, "Netflix, a proven factor in the success of healthy relationships."

"They could use that in their advertisements," I say. "You're so much fun. I can't believe how much fun you are. Are you sure you're even real?"

"Exactly as real as you are."

The existences belonging to every plane of being, up to the highest Dhyan-choyans, are, in degree, of the nature of shadows cast by a magic lantern on a colourless screen; but all things are relatively real, for the cogniser is also a reflection, and the things cognised are therefore as real to him as himself.

“I have to go back to Mexico, Kassandra. They’re the only ones who can fix this tooth.”

“What’s this really about, Dad?”

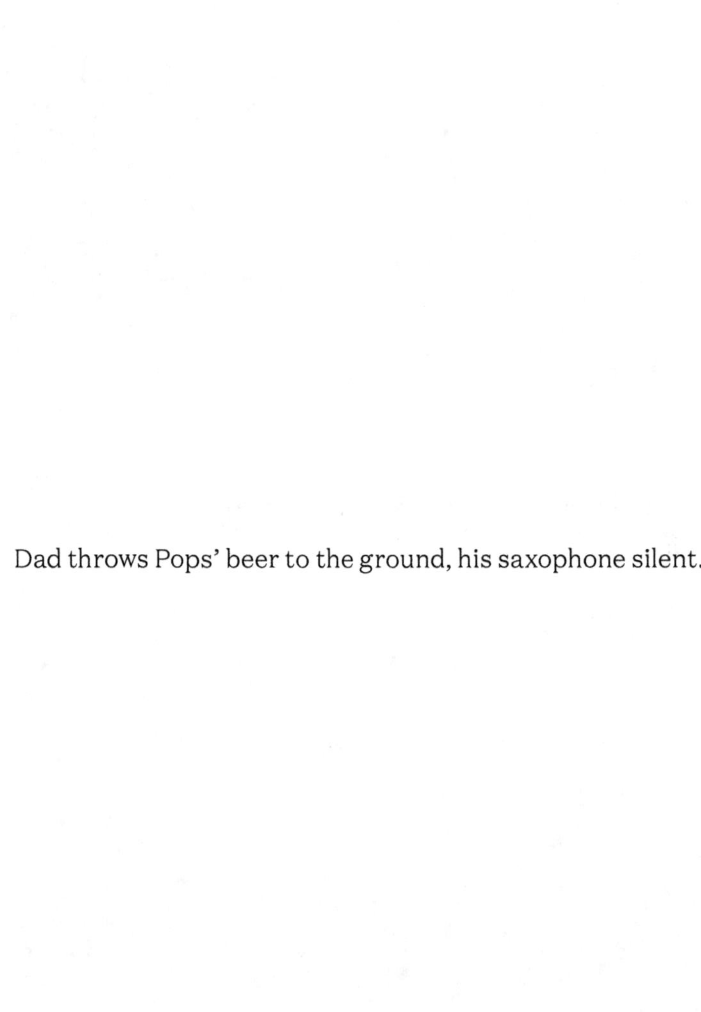

Dad throws Pops’ beer to the ground, his saxophone silent.

“Not too far under, and not too far over.”

“Not too far under, not too far over.”

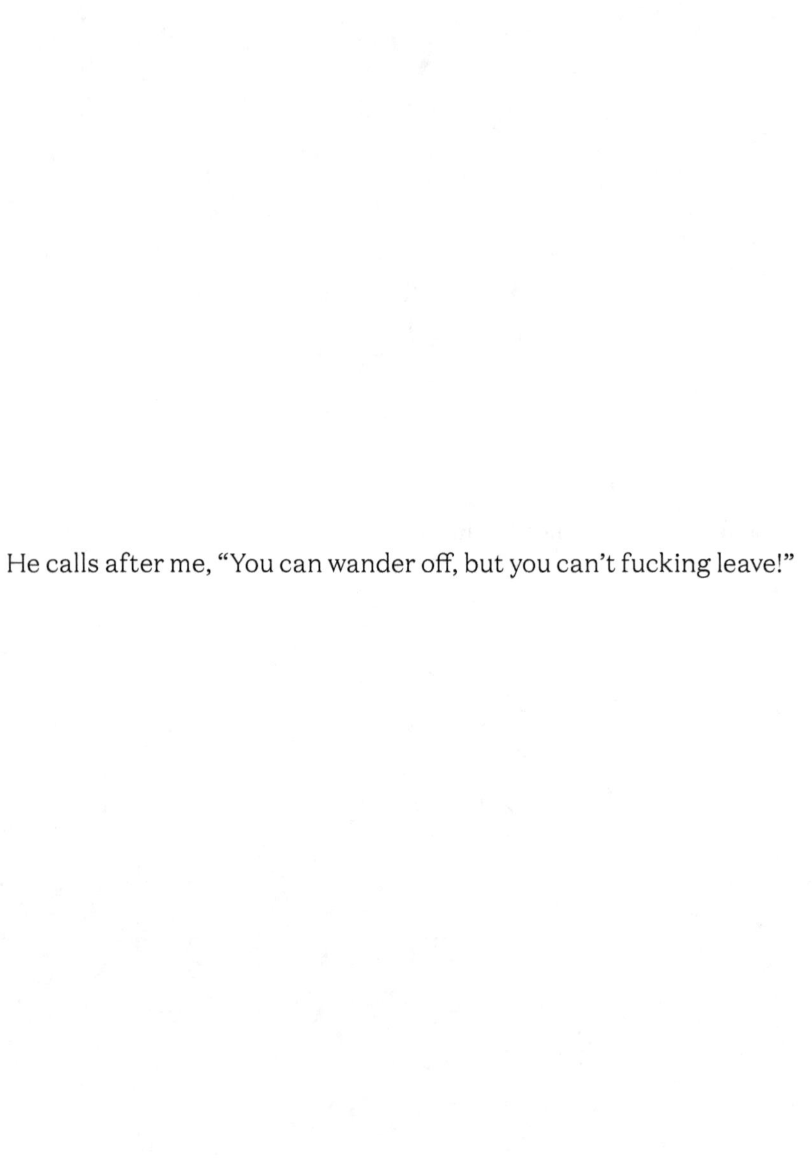

He calls after me, “You can wander off, but you can’t fucking leave!”

Sunday: When I... This is (laughter)... This is Magi 1. When I had the urge to make a statement by roaring up to David in the beautiful truck that God's blessed me with and my beautiful life that God's blessed me with and my beautiful wife that God's blessed me with, I had no idea… No idea… oh mi poor amor, no (indistinct attempts at Spanish in a tearful voice).

(Voice returns to normal) Both of our little niños are playing together on God's playground in the realms. Together. For love. And… and King David, uh, this is seven hours after his speech of double-barreled prayer badass shit. He's gotta message 'cause we're about ready to part company and we've had a great day, haven't we David?

Dad

Today 4:02 PM

Lonely

Lonely

Lonely

Lonely

Lonely

Lonely

Lonely

Lonely

"So, one of my daughters must have been really worried about me," he says, looking at me, "because someone called the cops while I was in John Day. But, before they got there, I was in the Best Western pool naked because there was no one around. I just wanted to swim naked in the pool where my baby girl swam naked all those years ago. And when the cops showed up, they told me to get out of the pool, told me my daughter had called, and asked to check my arms for track marks. Didn't have any. You know what they did when they saw I was naked? They just laughed. They told me not to drive until I was sober and took me to lunch! Gave me their business cards and said that, if I needed anything before I left town to give them a call! Put *that* shit in the book."

His last couple words come out with a strange quality, and it is a full 10 seconds before anyone realizes one of his teeth had fallen out onto the table.

Picking it up, he says, "Don't get in fights after dental surgery. PSA for you."

four six seven

seven

seven

By and between the 31st of March 2017 and April 1, 2017, Defendant sent several text messages to L   that say the following:

John

Fri, Mar 31, 10:23 PM

I might lose everything while you sit on your ass and do nothing to help? Nice, what assholes. Throw me in Jail, insane asylum while I work my ass off for you to persecute me over and over again so I can try to care for you? What appreciation. You could at least come to Utah and help me try to save us. If I had you I could pull this off. Your ego and jealousy amaze me. I want you to be happy, you want me to pay for your heaven and be in hell? How does that work in your head and heart? Christlike? Wow! Wake up and help me save you.

Fri, Mar 31, 11:47 PM

Have Dr   write another letter about how

awful I am

Sat, Apr 1, 2:46 AM

Fine, I will do it alone.   it has always been me and you leeches. I am human. Your protective order looks more and more stupid and malicious by the minute, I look better and better at being a husband and father. I fell down, you stay down, I get back up—no one cares.

Dad

Today 7:32 AM

<message>
<body>Just+talked+to+King+David%2C+he+got
+his+wife+out+and+they+are+back+in+Pendleton
.++He+found+handy+man+work+to+trade+for+a+
motel+room+and+they+are+panhandling+for+fo
od%2C+all+in+all+they+are+in+a+good+spot.++
%0A%0AMy+methods+might+be+unsavory+and
+at+times+unkind+but+my+heart+is+golden+an
d+my+intentions+are+pure.%0A%0AIf+you%27re
+gonna+cross+the+desert%2C+you%27ve+got+
to+have+a+reason+and+you%27ve+got+to+have
+a+vision+of+what+it+looks+like+when+you+are
+across+%28lets+go+see+the+fish+%3A%29
</body>
<date>1487011586165</date>
<read>1</read>
<type>1</type>
</message>

I'm looking as if through a camera lens at the place where consciousness began. There is a garden and water. There is a tangible potential energy about the place. As I watch, a flower shape blooms outward and asks to be noticed. It calls with an ache that is impossible to ignore, so I say, wordlessly, *I'm here. I'm here. I see you. I am noticing you. I recognize you. Thank you for being here.* In the room my body is still in, I distantly hear someone say, "Isn't she a lovely creature?" I hear the sound of the singing bowl but perceive it as color. I know it always begins with noticed and noticer.

∞

"There's something I can connect to sometimes, something reaching back to me or through me. Maybe it's a future version of me or an entity I don't understand, but something is reaching back through my timeline, and maybe everyone's timelines, to maneuver through possibilities. And I know what it tastes like, what it feels like."

"I know you do. I can feel it on you. It changes you and your intensity. It's magnetic."

"It's difficult to imagine being able to survive anymore without it. If it was just suddenly gone, if I didn't know what it felt like anymore, I think I would lose everything."

"For some of us, that's all there is."

∞

"In this state of mind, I'm living in all of them simultaneously. And living in them might even be synonymous with creating them. But, if we were to go back to living in just one...just one. I don't want to live in just one. But the way I see them right now, the way I see them, so many of them are ending, these realities are ending all the time. The world is always ending. All the doomsayers are right. And wrong. At the same time. Because there's always one that keeps going. But I can feel them. I can feel each of them as they leave. It's like they pass through me," I say.

"The world is ending, and time is repeating itself to try to stop it."

The sun is out
it melts the snow that fell yesterday
makes you wonder why it bothered

I need you here and not here too

but at least I author my own disaster

It's like we weren't made for this world
though I really wouldn't want
to meet someone
who was

Let's just have some fun
Let's tear this shit apart
Let's tear the fucking house apart
Let's tear our fucking bodies apart

Even Apocalypse is fleeting
there's no death
no ugly world
No matter where we are
we're always touching by underground wires

and none of our secrets are physical

I attend a full-moon meditation on the second floor of a food co-op. The guide asks me to imagine being led into a forest by an animal. In following this animal, I travel to the oldest, tallest tree in the forest, which I then climb until I am at the top and summon a great bird to take me to the stars.

Once in the vastness of the dark sky, the guide tells me to imagine asking the bird to take me to my celestial parents, wherever they may be, whatever they may look like. The guide wants me to listen to what they tell me, to see what they want me to see, to accept a gift from them.

I arrive at a large space rock upon which my celestial parents sit. My celestial mother's body is obscured in dark cloth, but her face, gray and purple, reminds me of a spider's face. My celestial father appears as a blocky white marble statue with the vague outlines of an older man with a long beard.

The spider-mother and statue-father give me a string of star pearls to wear around my neck to amplify my ideas. They tell me, "The time for being quiet is over."

Waking from a dream, I say, "I know what 343 is about!"

"Do you?"

"It's not about the number. It's about the pattern. Something is teaching me how to see it."

"Let's do it now. Right here. I don't want to wait anymore."

"Maybe now's not the best time with everything going on. Shouldn't we..."

"Wait? How much time do we have left? How much time does anyone have left?" I ask.

Eve sits up straighter and collects herself. "Will you take me to be your lifelong partner for what we know of eternity?" Eve asks.

"Would you take me?"

"Yes."

"Then, yes."

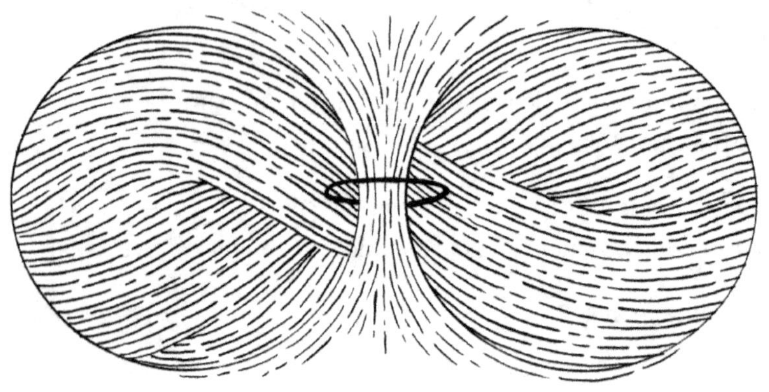

"Want to just start at the beginning?" the university therapist asks.

"Well, back a few months ago when I originally made the appointment, all the characters in my stories started dying. I couldn't sleep until I got up and wrote them down. And I couldn't even use the stories. They were just fragments. I thought I needed help.

"But then I met someone. And, I've been able to talk through a lot of this. I've been sleeping through the night."

"It sounds like you're doing much better."

"Yeah, I think so."

"So, why are you here?"

"Is it too early to love?" Eve asks.

“Don’t let him backslide, okay? My dad just got clean, and then, well, and then this happened. I’m just worried about him.”

“Look, I’ve been in contact with his sponsor. John’s stronger now than he was then. He still has all you kids to think about. I have complete faith in him.”

∞

“Thank god. Oh, thank god,” Pops says, “You don’t know what it’s been like, what it’s been like. Been up for three days. Slept in a diesel truck that night! Ain’t that right?”

Pops: I’m sorry, John. I’ve had a couple drinks, is all.

John: You’re a fuckin’ alcoholic. Got me started on this shit again. I’m going to . . . I’ll fuckin’ kill you for that. I just . . . I wanted a cello in the recording. And now all we have is your goddamn sax.

"This plane is coming in low and fast! Low and fast!"

"If I don't make it through this, you have to write the book, Kassandra. I have some money saved away for you—no one even knows about it—just promise me . . . "

∞

"I'm sorry. I'm sorry," I say.

"What's wrong? What happened?"

∞

"I didn't even know his real name."

Sunday: And we can't do no wrong. As long as we . . . as long as we're praising Jesus while we're being naughty, there's nothing we can do wrong. And that . . . that sucks for people who don't get that.

∞

"Look, I know what you've done. You don't have to admit it. And if you don't give back the $100,000 by tomorrow at 5 p.m., well, I know where your kids go to school. I know where your kids go to school."

I close my eyes and suck on the inside of my lips as I inhale sharply through my nose. "There are times when . . . well, given everything that's happened, sometimes I think . . . sometimes I think . . . it might just be easier if he . . . if he just died. If my dad just died already."

"I think you would hardly be human if you hadn't thought that at least once," Eve tells me, "but for what it's worth, I'm glad he didn't."

AFFADAVIT OF O Y

I responded quickly to the scene

before Defendant left, he had ripped down the tassels in the home

indicated to me that the victim's left ear had blood on it as if Defendant had ripped his earring out. I inspected the wounded area and saw that there was no earring and that there was blood. The victim told me that the Defendant wanted to kill him, but too many people would be mad

said Defendant had made him take his clothes off

heard Defendant talk about going to the border that night

stated that Defendant had head-butted him on the front of his forehead. Victim said that Defendant head-butted him without grabbing his head

stated that Defendant threw "booze" on him and then threw a lit cigarette onto him. Victim then went on to say that Defendant kept telling him that he was going to kill him. Victim became very emotional and said that if his brother had not been there, Defendant probably would have

Chief went to speak to Defendant's wife about relocating to a safe area for the night since Defendant had been thought to be on foot and had not been located.

I do believe this incident shows that Defendant is a danger to himself and others.

"Where do you think he's going to go?"

"The border, maybe? That would make sense. He could probably get across without a license, but that would be the end. He wouldn't be able to get back over. That would be the last we would hear of him."

"How do you feel about that?"

"What if we do get him help and he gets better? What then? He starts another family, gets stable, and in a couple years, this just starts all over again?"

Dad

Today 1:43 AM

Happy and homeless, albeit freezing, on Good Friday. The “rapture” prophecy is finally almost over. I have no money, no food, no ID, and I am sleeping up against a—gulp!—Catholic Church in Fort Collins. Exactly as all predicted, I would lose everything by Easter. I am supposed to attend mass at a Catholic Church in Latin America, not North America.

You could fly to Denver and drive me there? I can’t fly. No ID.

The last part of what I had to give up was my son, through my actions, NOT just giving Papa God my only begotten son willingly. I have suffered a great deal more than I needed to. But Wednesday night at midnight, I released him as well—hardest thing I have ever done, like Abraham putting Isaac on the altar.

In early terms, I cross, I never come back.

Today 1:52 AM

If you care about how I am doing, please fly to Denver asap, rent a car, drive 1 hour to Fort Collins

And
Drive me
To
The
Border—you can cross with me
Or
Be released from further obligation.

Easter Sunday will be bigger than the first one?

Dad

Today 1:58 AM

You could literally restore my thoughts of humanity and family single-handedly by "returning me" to my manger and saying goodbye

The lies being spread about me for most of my life are soon to be exposed.

You can tell anyone you want about my current state of affairs, but it would be a final act of Betrayal if you told my location to ANYONE but Eve.

I don't want help with anything else. If I could cross naked that would be perfect, but that would be being crazy "just for the sake of the book." Anyway, just a silly ride south, as quickly as possible, and a kiss—oops, you don't like my touch.

You could even send me money anyway, no ID is part of my "problem." "Prophecy."

Today 2:15 AM

Would it be weird if it WAS you? After all the other betrayers failed Me, I was sure the Last One was Judas. The one I thought would finally come through last night caused my first official night of homelessness.

Ouch—the final Judas.

No? Well, tell Z she is my only daughter. Kick life in the ass, Z.

AFFIDAVIT

Chief and I did locate multiple exits from which Defendant could have escaped without us noticing. Chief and I spoke with the owner of the bar. We asked if we could review the surveillance videos

granted us access to the video, but found that his videos had stopped recording around 12 P.M. that day.

"There's a lot of vagrant activity at that location, so it's likely that you're right about where he is if he was on foot," the officer tells me.

"St. John's, really?" Mom asks. "He would."

"If he were just going to book it to Mexico, I wouldn't call the police. But, he's hesitating. He's talking about fighting for his son. I don't want to worry about this anymore."

My phone rings at 11 p.m. I sit up in the dark, look at Eve, and grab her hand before answering.

"Hello?"

"Kassandra?"

"This is she."

"I'm calling to let you know that we have John in custody. He resisted and tried to run, but we made the arrest."

"Okay. Thank you for your help and for letting me know."

"You're welcome. Happy Easter."

∞

four six seven

seven

seven

"He posted bail."

"Where is he?"

"Since he had no place to stay in Wyoming, they allowed him to go to Idaho to stay with his aunt."

There is a momentary silence on the other end of the line.

"You know this doesn't mean it all has to happen again, right?"

"'In eternity, it is already accomplished,'" I say.

∞

My jerky, mechanical movements increase as Eve and I near the tent, now seizure-like in intensity. I hold my lower abdomen and brace against Eve's arm for support as I slump down on the half-inflated air mattress, my head in the corner of the tent furthest from the zippered door.

I lie on my back with both hands clasping my stomach, and even though it is still concave, each muscle underneath is heavy with the strain of movement as I splay my legs in a birthing position.

The darkness inside the tent is heavy. The blanket of night descends to make my thoughts thick as they circle the air around us. The spasms increase, but I stop paying attention to them because there are so many images flooding my mind. I see myself straddling a black hole, and the gravity of the black hole makes it possible for me to pull all the kinks out of my body. I see all bodies as cylinders and all babies birthed as a twisting off of their mothers not unlike rows of sausages.

I wonder if this is what God punished women with. Maybe there was never any twisting off and no loss of identity at all.

I see my parents, and I see how my story is the same as their stories. It's a reflection, a mirror. In living, I am completing them as I complete myself.

But I cannot continue down that line of thought because color unfolds and explodes behind my eyes, images of strings and lines interweaving and the fountain, the ever-present fountain shape. But, no, it's not a fountain; it's the structure of everything electromagnetic. I recognize it. It's not a funnel or a fountain; it's a toroidal field.

I term the Immortal one a plásmate, because it is a form of energy; it is living information. It replicates itself—not through information or in information—but as information . . . As living information, the plásmate travels up the optic nerve of a human to the pineal body. It uses the human brain as a female host in which to replicate itself into its active form. This is an interspecies symbiosis.

"So, wait, this plásmate thing. Is that really what's happening with us?"

"If a benevolent force were invading our world, the best place to hide is in plain sight."

"Inside us?"

"Yes."

"Like, an alien intelligence? I mean, this isn't science fiction."

"It doesn't have to be alien. Ideas are contagious. They live in our minds."

This is what we should look for. It's not for your elucidation, it's not part of your self-directed psychotherapy. You are an explorer, and you represent our species, and the greatest good you can do is to bring back a new idea because our world is in danger by the absence of good ideas. Our world is in crisis because of the absence of consciousness. And so to whatever degree any one of us can bring back a small piece of the picture and contribute it to building a new paradigm, then we participate in the redemption of the human spirit.

DNA
Microtubules
Toroidal field
Electromagnetic field (Earth's and
in the brain)
Christian fish symbol
Double helix
Black holes
Christian fish
Christian
            fish
Let's go see the fish

"All I'm getting is this strange feeling. Almost as if, as if you wanted to tell them...they aren't different. But more than that, that they're . . ."

" . . .connected. But not just connected, they're . . ."

" . . .inhabited."

"What does that mean to you?"

"There's something, something inside of me, inside of all of us. It might not even be human. It's almost like my consciousness . . ."

" . . .has nothing to do with me. I wanted to tell them . . ."

" . . .that they are not their consciousnesses. They are more than the sum of their parts. They are . . ."

" . . .not completely human. And you wanted to wake them up to it. You wanted to tell them . . ."

" . . .none of this is real or if it is . . ."

" . . .then there's something more real living inside us, controlling us, symbiotically inhabiting us. I found a part of it, and now you have it, too."

"'A hallucination is a species of reality.'"

"'What's to be gotten over is the false idea that a hallucination is a private matter.'"

"Don't . . . don't leave me alone."

"I never have."

"I need a piece of paper," Eve says.

Eve writes "343" and flips it upside down before handing it back to me.

"Look."

343

"What? Eve? Shit." I laugh.

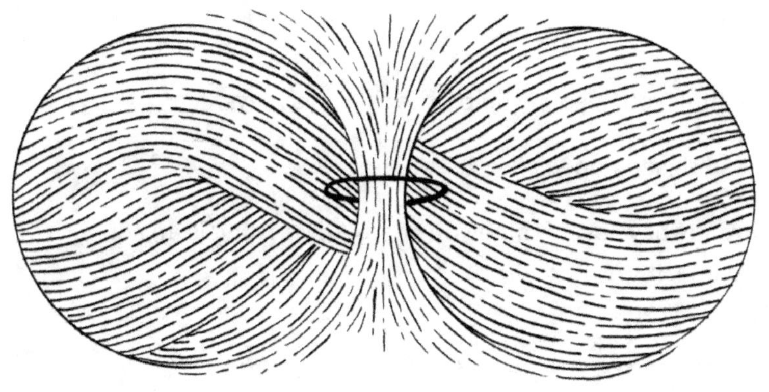

“I don’t think you need my help,” the therapist says.

“Do I need to see a specialist, or . . . ?”

“You already have everything you need. All learning is an act of remembering.”

∞

It seems that, sooner or later, we'll have to give up on the fallacy of the continuity of self. We are not the same person, physically—in terms of our cells—as we were seven years ago. And where do we draw the line? When do we say, "I am no longer what I was" when the reconstruction is continual? We are perpetually in the process of destroying and recreating ourselves. We are ships with the same name but ever-changing parts.

"Your dad wrote a song, and F is putting up decorations. I thought maybe you could write a poem. We could hang it up on his wall once he gets home from the hospital to make him feel welcome. And Eve can come, too."

"He'll be home in a week, right?" I ask.

"If you can't do it, that's all right. I just thought you might want to."

"I'd love to."

∞

"That's what real love looks like, huh, Mom?"

∞

"I want to be a body of words."

"That'd be a neat Halloween costume."

"I don't want to wait that long."

"Do you think it's okay to cut this quote short?"

"You're the artists."

"Should we include the quotation marks?"

"You're the artists."

"Stop crying. You'll smear the ink."

"Kassandra, I hate to be the one to tell you this, but your dad fell down the stairs at his aunt's house. He hit both sides of his frontal lobe. I'm not sure if he's going to pull out of it. He doesn't remember who he is. He doesn't remember his name."

"Are you okay, Dad? Dad?"

"We did it; we landed the plane," he says.

"What are you talking about?"

"There's a time when you want intimacy with the people around you, when you want them to understand without the translation, but there's also a time to be clear. It's cruel that, when you are pushed to your emotional limits, that's when you most need to know the difference between the two."

"Just lay back, Dad. Just rest."

∞

Dad

Today 3:38 PM

I wouldn't put it past the universe that this 'injury' was for my own good in the long run. Slower prefrontal cortex and a diminished midbrain might be just what I needed. I am currently way above average on cognitive skills—the doctors can't believe that, still weak and tired, though. I was caught in between a desperate attempt to be understood and appreciated and a strong defiance to that being easy . . . without really understanding.

"I have no idea what's real anymore, but I'm not sure I need to know."

"Try having a traumatic brain injury. You can't trust anything."

∞

At the front of the auditorium, I stand in front of lecture slides. I briefly look at where Eve sits in the audience before continuing, "In a simulation, you don't keep failed solutions around. Every time a possible solution is proven nonviable, you can stop spending resources searching that possibility out. You save computing power. But, you don't want to start all the way over; you want to start back to where that solution didn't work. And why create new consciousnesses to experiment with? That would create too many new variables. No, you want to reload the same consciousnesses and make them believe the simulations are seamless.

"And, you wouldn't want your simulation to happen in real time; that would be too slow. You need a way to trick your simulated consciousnesses to think time has passed. And why not have multiples of their timelines going at once?

"It's currently impossible to know for sure that we, ourselves, are living in a simulation, so we have to operate under the assumption that we aren't. But, if we are in a simulation, say one designed to find out where we don't destroy ourselves through climate change, nuclear war, or overpopulation, then there's the possibility that things will get better, more peaceful, more livable for larger groups of people. More rights, more diversity, more understanding. And the ability to improve upon those improvements is limitless.

Within all this, everything that happens is necessary for our survival. 'In eternity, it is already accomplished.'"

It’s been a week since the idea birth, and I feel empty. There is no movement at the center of me, but lying down to take a nap, I dimly hear a voice I recognize.

“Do you want another one?”

Without any hesitation, I respond even as I feel the air grow charged and *full.*

“Yes.”

∞

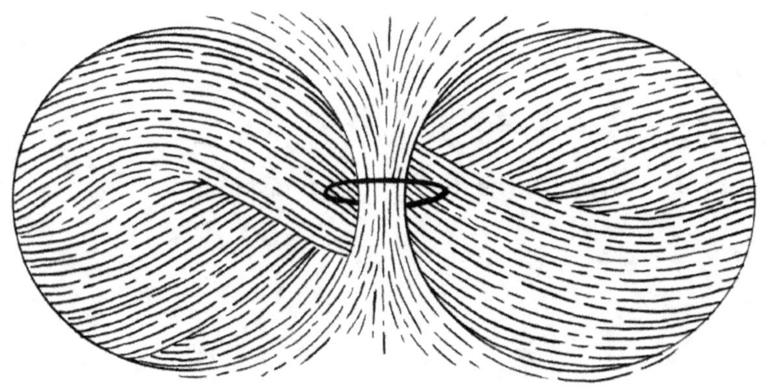

“Want to just start at the beginning?” the university therapist asks.

CITATIONS

"Up on Cripple Creek, she sends me . . ."
"Up on Cripple Creek" by The Band

"I never meant to cause you any sorrow . . ."
"Purple Rain" by Prince

"Shamans in all times and places gain their power . . ."
Terence McKenna

"The monkeys . . . they laugh because it hurts so much."
Stranger in a Strange Land by Robert A. Heinlein

"Wide Sargasso Sea *references supernatural stories . . ."*
Wide Sargasso Sea by Jean Rhys

"Our brain is not a stand alone information processing organ . . ."
Abstract of "Consciousness in the Universe in Scale Invariant and Implies and Event Horizon of the Human Brain" by Dirk K. F. Meijer and Hans J. H. Geesink

"Everything has been called into question . . ."
Robber Bride by Margaret Atwood

"The great secret known to Apollonius of Tyana, John of Tarsus . . ."
VALIS by Philip K. Dick

"Love, beyond providing emotional sustenance, compassion . . ."
Mating in Captivity by Esther Perel

"Language has made us more than a group of pack-hunting . . ."
Terence McKenna

". . . brings, brings, thus, the poem . . ."
Voyaging Portraits by Gustav Sobin

"The existences belonging to every plane of being . . ."
The Secret Doctrine, Volume I by Helena Blavatsky

"The sun is out it melts the snow that fell yesterday . . ."
"The Past is a Grotesque Animal" by Of Montreal

"In eternity, it is already accomplished."
VALIS by Philip K. Dick

"I term the Immortal one a plásmate . . ."
VALIS by Philip K. Dick

"This is what we should look for. It's not for your elucidation . . ."
Terence McKenna

"A hallucination is a species of reality."
VALIS by Philip K. Dick

"What's to be gotten over is the false idea that a hallucination . . ."
Terence Mckenna

ACKNOWLEDGMENTS

To the people who find their likenesses here, I hope I opened portals to healing for you. Thank you for letting me use your words.

To Dane, you were a glowing light shining through a dimming body. I will never forget your name.

“Three Days” first appeared in *Mapping Salt Lake City*.

∞

K. M. LIGHTHOUSE graduated from the University of Utah and worked as the senior poetry director of *enormous rooms* for two years but has since made the Pacific Northwest a home. The poet's other works appear in *From Sac*, *Blue Lake Review*, and *Toasted Cheese,* as well as two chapbooks entitled *You Are an Ambiguous Pronoun* and *The Observer Effect*. K. M. Lighthouse is an assistant organizer with Portland's Eastside Poetry Workshop and a member of High Priestesses of Poetry.

www.ingramcontent.com/pod-product-compliance
Lightning Source LLC
Chambersburg PA
CBHW070421010526
44118CB00014B/1851

* 9 7 8 0 9 9 7 2 9 8 7 7 2 *